Aging Like a Guru

...Who Me?

By

Dr. Rosie Kuhn

Aging Like a Guru

First published in the United States by The Paradigm Shifts Publishing Co.

PO Box 1637, Eastsound WA 98245

Cover design & formatting by Maureen O'Neill, at On Fire Coaching.

(Fonts: Adobe Trajan, Trajan Pro and Microsoft Calibri),

Edited by Jessica Ruby Hernandez, at Lotus Glow.

ISBN: 978-0-9908151-1-2

Dedication

I dedicate this book to all human beings. We are all aging gurus.

Table of Contents

Introduction

Aging – Who Me?

If you are old enough to be reading this book, you are old enough to understand that you have been participating in the aging process well before your little feet landed on the planet. You experienced the process of aging when you lost your first teeth around the age of six. Six years later, you began to develop muscle, breasts, pubic hair, and growth. Invisible hormones began to create sensations that were way beyond your ability to control. For many of us, we looked forward to these changes. For others, not so much!

In the mid-thirties and forties, you begin to notice a wrinkle or two, and grey hair begins to pop up in the most peculiar places. Perhaps the biological clock is ticking, pressing upon you the need to get started with baby-making, if you haven't already.

In the late forties and into your fifties, your skin begins to loosen and get crepe-y. Boobs sag - and so does everything else. Erections are more difficult, and so is peeing. Little by little you experience physical changes that you heard were coming, but always believed it would never happen to you. Who me?

I recently gave a talk at the Orcas Island Senior Center regarding aging and independence. In that hour and a half, those who attended began to share what it was really like inside themselves, and how they were participating - willingly or not, in the process of aging. No one minced words or used languaging that lightens the reality that life, as we knew it, had changed dramatically, and that there is no way out of this aging process!

What was shared was the degree of denial that many of us live in: the kind of denial that robs us of freedom of choice. What was also shared was the degree to which so many of us isolate ourselves, because we believe that we are the only ones going through the emotional upheavals of the process of aging.

When we look around at how others are being with aging, it appears as if everyone else has a handle on it. One person offered to the group; "I'm afraid that if I share what aging is really like for me, people will decide there is something definitely wrong with me. So I isolate. I don't want people to see me as old and decrepit. I figure I'll fake it till I make it!"

So, consider every individual - especially women in their early adulthood (30's and 40's), who utilize plastic surgery to avoid and distract themselves from the natural progression and evolution of their being, physical and otherwise. Each of us, in our own way, is attempting to fake it till they make it. They want to hold at bay the inevitable annihilation of the "ME" we imagine ourselves to be. But, who are we really? Perhaps we are already who we are pretending to be? How can we know unless we do a little exploring of who is inside this soon-to-be, if not already, bag of bones?

With aging, regardless of which stage of life we are talking about, there is a metamorphosis process that is taking place. In truth, it scares the Bejeesus out of each and every one of us. Why? Because we don't know how to do this thing called life. We would rather practice tried-and-true DENIAL: Don't Even Know I Am Lying. Who wants to admit to themselves, or to anyone else, the degree to which they feel powerless and helpless about the changes occurring to them and in them? Um, like, no one!

Johnny Depp says "I don't know how to be a grownup - I've never done it before." None of us know how to do aging. Even those who consider themselves experts in the field - they too have to have their own personal and direct experience of aging, for better or worse, to truly understand and know aging.

Each of us is here for the opportunity to figure out who we are as we transition through each developmental stage of aging. You are not alone! And though, it may look as if this stage of aging isn't going to end well, the truth is that it will be what you make of it!

The other day, at a second gathering of individuals curious enough to continue the discussion on aging at the Senior Center, one of the participants declared: “It’s not an adventure if you couldn’t die doing it.” Who is up for an adventure? Okay, most of us aren’t so thrilled with the idea that death is possible when facing an adventure. However, in this particular adventure called Your Life, death is not only a possibility, it is inevitable.

What I want for each individual on the planet is to experience the fulfillment of their human-spirit. Cultivating the awareness that each of us has the capacity to empower ourselves to make that happen, well, that is a responsibility that comes with experience - through aging.

None of us will get out of here with our human suits on. It’s as though we are on a business trip, here on Earth, to get the job done. Then, we get to go home. But what is the job to be done? I have no doubt that you know what’s yours to do. And, well, you get to decide how you will proceed, given the tasks at hand.

Where Do We Go From Here?

What you will find within the covers of this book are short stories, narratives, and anecdotes about people and stages of their lives. Each focuses on a particular aspect of life as we age. The intention of this book is to provide a perspective and some encouragement to examine and explore who you are in the midst of this human experience, regardless of where you are in the aging process. This isn’t a how-to book, per se. It is more of a how it is, and a how it can be, book.

Sure, it may seem that we are attempting to make lemonade out of lemons, but why not? We’ve got all the lemons in the world - maybe we can make a pie or two while we are at it!

I love the saying of John Lennon: “Everything is great in the end. If it’s not great, it’s not the end!” What a great reminder!

Aging like a guru requires us to get acquainted with who is inside these beautiful vehicles of life - our bodies. It requires that we see the humor and delight that travels along with us. And, to age like a guru requires the practice of seeing that, as my dad always said up until he died at age 91, it just gets better every day!

Chapter One

Is This as Good as It Gets?

Most of us expect that when we age we will decline in every way possible. We hold firm to the belief that this is the way it is supposed to be, and we blindly walk down the path of decline. But if that is the truth, why do some people actually thrive as they age? What's up with that?

Taking inventory of the Good, the Bad, the Beautiful, and the sometimes Ugly, while driving down the highway, I see old cars in pristine shape, and wonder how it is that those things still run. Obviously, somebody takes really good care of them - that's how! Someone dotes and primps on their well-oiled machine in order to keep it that way. I admire those people for their dream, their vision, and their passions – it keep their car looking great, and it keeps them challenged and excited about life.

Our bodies are much like those cars. I think that most of us have a lot more miles available - especially since so many of our parts can be replaced. It doesn't take a lot of fine-tuning; just a bit of pedal-to-medal every once in a while, to keep the pipes from clogging up. So what keeps us in the mindset of allowing ourselves to rust out, as it were, and end up in the junk yard? Yuck, that isn't a happy thought, is it?

We would like to believe that miraculous transformation will restore us to our original luster and beauty. Sadly though, even miracles take some effort to pull off, and so most of us decide we just don't want to do it anymore.

The Mechanics Handbook

It is easier than ever these days to go onto the Internet, type in a question about aging and change, and BAZINGA! We have tons of information to sift through. Some of it provides worst-case scenarios; some of it is best-case scenarios. Are we victims of aging, or are we continually empowered to make empowering choices? Our presumptions set the stage for our experience. Our experience reinforces our presumptions, which cultivates ruts, and now we are not only victims to aging, but we are also victims to our ruts.

I Can't Get out of My Rut - Another Presumption

You may like your rut. It's comfortable; change isn't required - just the willingness to see life within your rut as, this is as good as it gets!

It's not necessarily true, it's just the truth you choose to live by and die by.

A few weeks ago, it was almost as if someone flipped the switch, and my fingers and knee joints began to hurt. "Ah, this is it," I decided. "This is the beginning of a life with arthritis. I won't be able to walk with Gracie. I'll have to ...." The worries and angst began to take up my day. Then, a nutritionist friend asked me if my diet had changed? I said yes, actually, and then shared with her what I was eating. She said that what I was eating was causing the inflammation which was causing the stiffness, which was causing the pain. "Stop eating so much of... and you'll probably see a huge difference in your body." She was right. In a matter of days, the pain is just about gone. It's a miracle! The only miracle here is that I chose to stop eating something that I enjoy. I stopped eating something that was causing me pain. That's not a miracle, that's just intelligence, eh?

I'm as likely as anyone to travel down the well-worn path of "truths," such as the favorite, that aging sucks. After all, I'm just a human being like everyone else. I, like everyone else, cling to the remnants of a life raft that takes me down the river of worry and fear that I'm getting older, and that that means pain and suffering. It's the best I can hope for. However, sometimes, to save yourself, you have to jump ship and swim for your life. Swimming for your life is an act of will, passion, and commitment. It takes courage to peel your grasping fingers from the rails of what you believe will save you, and surrender into the waters of faith. It might be true that either way you are going down, so only you get to decide how you want to go down.

How can we prepare for this inevitable journey of aging when it is such an individual experience? We are trained to hope for the best but expect the worst. Shifting the weight of attention from what is being taught and what we have learned, to what we know and has never been forgotten, we begin again to empower ourselves to live the life that is full of delicious richness as we embrace our aging process.

Preprogrammed Automation

While we watch the news and commercials, and just about every page on the Internet, we are bombarded by information and ads that continue to reinforce that we are just cogs in the wheel of life. Do this. Don't do that. Be afraid - be very afraid!

And, I don't know one single person who says "Hey, I want to be a cog in the wheel. I want to be led down the primrose path by the ring in my nose. I want to get all rusted out and end up in a junk yard." Yet, here we are, preprogrammed automatons, most of us doing what we think we should do, or resisting doing what we want to do. Whoopee!

Aging like a guru requires looking at how we choose to see who we are in this experience called life. We begin to notice how we choose to look at life, circumstances, and our thoughts, feelings, needs and wants, in relation to life.

Aging like a guru allows us to notice that judging ourselves and others doesn't really help us become happy and healthy. Each of us have our own way of viewing the world and living it. There is no right way, wrong way, or good or bad way. That's just the way it is!

Sometimes, all I can do is declare that aging sucks! Anguish, fear and pain nurture the suckiness of my experience. When I think of how gurus age, I imagine that they just shrug their shoulders, take a deep breath, and relax into the moment. Rather than declare that this current episode of suckiness is as good as it gets, they remind themselves that this too shall pass.

Chapter 2

If I Weren't Me

A favorite part of my job as a Life Coach is that I get to witness human beings take tiny filaments of beliefs and turn them into huge knots of limitations. They, like most of us, aren't able to hear themselves speak, nor see how their thoughts create the world around them. As their thinking partner, I hear what they themselves can't hear, and I share with them what I'm hearing so that they can make sense of the tangled knots of beliefs that stir within. After which they are at choice to choose differently.

The other most favorite part of my job is witnessing people courageously untangle those knotted up filaments of beliefs and weave them into a magnificent tapestry of fulfillment and joy.

My client Shirley is in her mid-fifties, and in our most recent session informed me, in every way but Sunday, that she would be better off being someone else, because if she was someone else, all of her circumstances would be good and easy. "If I weren't me, I wouldn't fail and I wouldn't suck at just about everything!"

Now Shirley is one of the most courageous and brilliant people I've ever had the honor to work with. Regardless of how brilliant one is, there are inherent beliefs that tie us into knots and limit our intelligence, wisdom, and the ability to see clearly enough to choose what is in the best interest for all involved.

Shirley is initiating an amazing startup company in Silicon Valley. She is also in relationship with a very challenging and dangerous horse. She isn't making progress with either the start up or the horse, and so, she sees herself as a failure. She says, "I would know what to do if I weren't me." Then, Shirley says, "What I want is to know what to do. What I want is to have the answers that would make all of this easier. Then it wouldn't be so obvious that I SUCK!"

Like most of us, Shirley looks outside of herself to see how others have successfully overcome these obstacles that are keeping her struggling with her challenges.

I'm not unfamiliar with this belief that *if I weren't me* life would be hugely different. So, I empathize with Shirley's dilemma. Her dilemma though, isn't whether she should put her horse down, who is not only dangerous but also lame, or whether she knows all the right answers to bring in funding for her startup. No, her dilemma is that, although she is Shirley and will always be Shirley, she can't reconcile this truth with the fact that she doesn't know how to be Shirley and be with the truths of what is. She doesn't know how to be in the midst of very challenging circumstances. The truth is, no one knows how to be in very challenging circumstances!

Shirley, like the rest of us, shuns, resists or shuts down the human experience of powerlessness, hopelessness, and helplessness. She hates feeling out of control. She hates herself when she is out of control. Raise your hand if you've never felt this way! Raise your hand if you are in denial of ever having felt this way! The point is, I don't know a single person that hasn't been, or isn't currently in Shirley's dilemma: *how do I be me while in the midst of such deep personal challenges?*

Shirley is facing a hugely common occurrence of being human: feeling powerless, helpless, and hopeless - AKA, feeling out of control. And, my experience is that most of us will do everything possible to avoid feeling out of control. We would rather blame, shame, hate and rage against ourselves than to accept that, due to the fact that we are human, we can't always know what to do, and we can't always know how to do what needs to be done. Sometimes life just sucks, and there is no way around it.

The statement "If I weren't me..." creates a type of insanity. Yes, it's true that if I weren't me I'd be somebody else. For some reason though, we believe that being someone else would mean we wouldn't have problems. Well, the truth is, you wouldn't perhaps have these problems, but you would definitely be facing other problems and dilemmas that would be just as challenging.

The constant barrage of challenges that are Shirley's, in this moment, are sourced in her core belief that being Shirley isn't enough - that she isn't enough. As she and I uncover this deep truth, Shirley sobs uncontrollably. In these deep moments of grief, she begins to reclaim herself. She sees that, over and over again, she has thrown herself under the bus: she denies her own experience of being powerless and helpless, and in doing so casts aside her own knowing and wisdom, and focuses on what other people are telling her to do.

As we grow, develop, unfold, and yes, age, we increase our capacity to listen with intelligence to what is being said inside our heads and inside our hearts. Aging gives us the opportunity to work out the truths of who we are and who we are not; we can see limiting beliefs and how they affect us. It's easier to see this in other people, and, quite often, we say "I'm glad I'm not her. I'm glad I'm not him. In this moment, I'm glad I'm me!"

No one likes facing the unknown. No one likes not knowing what to do. No one likes feeling vulnerable within those life circumstances that wring us of every shred of smartness, and right-action. These moments are the big Fat Be-With's of life, within which we surrender our "if only's," and our "what I want is", and be with what is - the *Is*ness of Is.

Admitting that we are powerless over our circumstance and over people, places, and things, empowers us to surrender to the truth of the moment, which, for Shirley is that *"It Sucks!"* The truth isn't that Shirley sucks as a human being; the truth is that her circumstance suck. She now gets to be with the *Big Fat Be With* of being Shirley. And, inevitably, she will know what to do, she will do it, and she will feel good about herself when all is said and done. That's what happens. Eventually we realize that we have the capacity to accept what we cannot change, the courage to change the things we can, and we have the wisdom to know the difference. Yes, this is the Serenity Prayer.

In the midst of our human challenges, even the most horrendous ones, we can look to anyone around us and know, without a doubt, that they too know what it's like to be in sucky circumstances. We are all so courageous. And at the same time, we are so afraid of discovering where our courage will take us. Wha-hoooo!

Aging like a guru allows us to feel the true human experience of what it is like to be in despairing situations. We feel all of what goes on within the

Big Fat Be With, denying nothing of this deep experience that can only be experienced by us, individually.

Aging like a guru also allows each of us to inevitably choose with gladness to choose to be “me.” In so doing, we begin to respect and honor the “me” that has gone through enormous amounts of adventures, has struggled, survived, and now has the capacity for greater wisdom and a greater capacity for happiness.

There comes a moment for each of us as we step into our guru-ness when we have access to being able to celebrate choosing to be exactly who we already are.

Chapter 3

The Aging Dreamer - the Ageless Dreamer

"There are literally no limits to what you may now choose to experience within the context of this physical form.... One must now take total responsibility for the focused intent that underlies one's choices." (Oneness, p.299)

As I read these words from my favorite book, *Oneness,* I ask myself the question - *What do people who are aging dream and imagine? What do I dream and imagine? Or, have I given up believing in dreams; that I'm too old to have my dreams come true?*

Dreaming and imagining are essential components of our human psyche. At every age, through stories, music, imagination and play, we cultivate the capacity to make believe: we make our believings into reality. We imagine ourselves as heroes and bad guys. We imagine ourselves as royalty ruling over our domains. We dream of being super-powered people, able to leap tall buildings in a single bound. Never do we dream of being depressed pathetic losers.

Dreaming, imagining, and fantasizing utilizes and strengthens our powers to create. Within our dreams we are inspired to make things happen. If you look around at everything that has been made by humans, it is all born out of creation, which is born out of imagining and dreaming. Science, music, philosophy, medicine... all of it comes from dreaming and imagining.

Quite often we stop dreaming and creating when something or someone tells us we can't make our dreams come true. We lose faith, and we lose trust in ourselves. We begin to think small and play small, and inevitably depression sets in; for after all, depression is what is left when we take away our powers to be the fullest expression of our essential selves.

My client Randall, when he was 13 years old, dreamed and imagined himself being a hugely successful musician. He had all the details worked out and he knew, without a doubt, that he would make his dream come true.

When he shared his dream with his dad, he was shattered by his father's ridicule and insults. Randal was told in no uncertain terms that the life of a musician wasn't something to strive for. His father told him to give up the dream. And, so he did.

Randall, being a creative person, found other outlets for his dreams and creativity, but, now in his 60's, he realizes the dream of singing and playing music has always been with him. The dream and the dreamer never died.

For decades, Randall put off allowing himself to even know his full capacity of making his dream come true. Today, he is beginning to put some muscle behind his intention, and has taken up a practice that will ultimately bring about the fulfillment of his dream. The most important part of this practice is taking full responsibility for the degree to which he will make it happen!

Some people would say - as Randall says himself, that it's too late, he doesn't have the resources, the time, or the sex appeal of youth, and that he will never know whether he would have been successful at fulfilling the dream of his childhood. Randal actually knows nothing about what's possible, and to a huge degree, it truly doesn't matter. What matters is that his dream wants expression in the real world, and Randall is committed to making that happen.

Whereas, in young children, there are no limits to our super-powers, as we progress and age, our imaginings become more logical and pragmatic. In our teens, we consider careers, schools, traveling, education, relationships, and what's going to make the most money. We create within imposed limits of possibility. We begin to make-believe based on what the "real world" reflects is possible and what is important. Our dreams begin to be shaped by what other people think and want, what's possible, affordable, and doable. We stop believing that everything, and I do mean everything, is possible.

In our 20's, 30's, and 40's it appears as if we are implementing the bones of our dreams and imaginings, and making them real. We get jobs, make money, some settle down, get married, have children. We plan for retirement. Many people are supposedly living the dream, but whose dream is it?

When we imagine ourselves, or actually be in our 50's, 60's and older, what do we dream and imagine? What is the stuff of our imagination? My hopes and wishes are not the same as my dreams. I hope to remain healthy; I hope I can sustain my lifestyle; I hope to see my children more regularly... These are not dreams. So what are my dreams?

That we dream is an essential core to our being human - not unlike breathing. That we have limitless capacity to not only dream but fulfill our dreams, is as plain as the petals on a flower. That we choose to limit our abilities to fulfill our dreams is only based on the interpretations within which we make believe. Here are some common beliefs I hear: "I'm too old; I don't have the resources; If I had more time I could; I'm going to fail; I'm afraid I am undeserving of having my dreams come true; What's the point of fulfilling a dream - where's it going to get me?; If I were someone else I know I could do it. And, one of my favorites: I only dream dreams that I know I can make happen."

It takes courage and strength, at every age, to take full responsibility for the focused intent that underlies the fulfillment of our dreams. To dream or not to dream doesn't matter so much as choosing to ask two questions: "Am I living my dream?" That's a scary one. The next question could be even scarier, depending on how you answered that first: "Am I willing to cultivate the courage and strength to dream, and to live into that, regardless of the outcome?"

I'm sitting with these two questions myself. They are stirring something within me. In this moment, I dream to be as courageous as Randall. Why? Because he is willing to risk facing his worst fears for the sake of experiencing the truest expression of himself. He knows the outcome will most likely not be the fame and fortune he dreamed of as a child, though, given his convictions, that is undoubtedly a huge possibility. Regardless of the outcome, he is going for it!

Aging like a guru brings possibility to every aspect of everyone's life. Limitations are like clouds in the sky that can be disappeared with intention and belief that everything is possible, yes, even if you're "old."

Aging like a guru allows us to look closely at our beliefs and the conditions within which we built those beliefs. We see how it made perfect sense for Randall to stop living his dream, given the conditions of the environment within which he was raised. We see how Randall now has the capacity to create conditions that allow him to live into his dream effortlessly. If we can see it for Randall, then we can begin to see it for ourselves.

Aging like a guru truly allows us to live the dream; we just have to discern what that dream is for each of us!

Chapter 4

Coming of Age – Regardless of Age

One theme of ***Aging - Who Me?*** is that we are never not aging. We are never not developing, growing, unfolding, and evolving. We are, in fact, in a constant state of emerging and unfolding.

As humans we are bombarded with choices constantly as our lives unfold. Some are big choices, and some, not so big. For example: An individual has to choose the right type of higher education for themselves after high school, or none; choose marriage or parenthood, or neither; choose the "right" career; choose to become a parent; choose how to be with family members who are harmful and abusive; choose how to be with an incurable disease, choose to come out of the closet in regard to their sexuality, their spirituality, or politics; choose to join the armed forces; choose how to follow a calling, inspirations or creativity that, to many, goes beyond avant-garde; and, choose how to face death. All of these have one question in common: who am I inside this experience, and how do I be true to myself in this choosing, no matter what!?

Life is a process of immersing ourselves into one dramatic and poignant story after another, based on the choices we make. Each story is filled with a unique and personal orientation and perspective - a maze of challenges which cultivate clarity of truth and knowing of what is one's highest truth and what is one's highest contribution to the world. Each could be considered a Rite of Passage.

Rites of Passage/Coming of Age - Regardless of Age

A Rite of Passage is a moment of individuating. Within an event or circumstance, an individual must allow themselves to have a true and authentic voice. Speaking the truth, however, first requires knowing the truth. And knowing the truth means that it is not amendable by what other people think, say or do. It is a point where you defer to no one.

In many Rites of Passage, there is a threshold, a crescendo - what the I-Ching calls reaching Critical Mass. In this moment, there is no not choosing. These moments of Critical Mass quite often are experienced as death-defying leaps.

A Rite of Passage, in essence, isn't some lovely ceremony that pronounces an individual grown up; in fact, the ceremony and celebration usually comes after the Rite of Passage has been completed. A Rite of Passage is a process through which one must travel - quite often alone. There is anguish and struggle, courage and strength, potential failure and despair. Insights and wisdom are born, as is a greater capacity to trust one's own ability to not only survive but to thrive. There is the working out of what is, and what is not; who is and who is not. There is a fight for life - sometimes physical life, but more often than not, it is the life of our essential self, leading to the fulfillment of our deepest expression of Self.

Aging, and all of the contributing aspects of the process, provides us with many Rites of Passage. What this means is that we face endings and changes continually, regardless of our age. In each ending and with each change we create a Rite of Passage. In what feels like a pivotal and critical moment, each of us chooses how to face what is directly confronting. How do each of us choose to be true and to trust ourselves, throughout this process? We choose by stepping into one moment at a time with care, vigilance, and hope that what happens next will bring about a positive outcome, no matter what!

In each of these moments, answers to critical questions can no longer be put off for another day. We have to discern and reveal answers to the questions: *In what ways have I ignored, avoided and distracted myself from my truth? Am I worthy of my own unique authentic expression? How do I be more honoring and honorable to myself in this current situation, this current life challenge? When death is at my door, how will I greet it?*

The beauty of these Rites of Passage is that they bring each of us to a deeper relationship with ourselves. We come to know our capabilities and our vulnerabilities. We learn to be humble in the face of powerlessness, hopelessness, and the inevitable truth, that we are human beings after all, with no extended warranty tag anywhere. We surrender our resistance in humility, and at the same time, discover a daringness that cannot be found any other way.

Aging like a guru takes us into adventures we never imagined for ourselves. Quite often, after all is said and done, we are grateful for these opportunities to truly experience the incredible resilience and wisdom that is within us, given the opportunity to reveal and trust our truest essential nature.

I'm asked quite often how my work as a transformational coach differs from therapy and other forms of coaching. I say that my work is to steward individuals through the process of becoming their truest and most authentic self. This means that, as their thinking partner, I empower them to cultivate awareness regarding how they perceive the world, and to trust their own way of seeing and being in the world. This means noticing when they choose to collapse into their fear and hide under their beds, and when they choose to make choices that serve only their highest truth and the fulfillment of their human spirit. Truthfully, though, people want transformation, but they don't want to change. Such is the dilemmas of our humanity.

Aging like a guru gives each of us plenty of opportunities to choose, then choose again. Inevitably, we begin to let go of the concept of failure and learn to accept what is. We learn that through our choosing, we discover a level of open acceptance, a deep knowing, great humility, and a comfort that somehow feels like home. Ain't it great that we will all arrive here, sooner or later? This is when we celebrate the fulfillment and completion of our Rites of Passage!

Chapter 5
Ah, Malaise

I woke up this morning sad, frustrated and disappointed. "Why?" I ask myself. "It's a beautiful day on Orcas, you are healthy, you have money in the bank and a lot of good friends." The me who is sad says, "Yes, I know, but…."

This is pretty much a lifelong pattern for me, of waking up in a mild malaise. I'm a regular Ginger Rogers when it comes to this unhappy song and dance. I'm on to me now, though, and can trip up this unhappy La-La-La more frequently than ever before.

The truth is that for decades I've been unaware of the underlying sensations that this malaise is thriving upon, not so much like a parasite, but sort of. Somewhat like a symbiotic relationship, but not quite that either.

Malaise is a beautiful word for "I'm feeling powerless, helpless, and hopeless, and I don't even know it, or for that matter, don't even want to know it." It is a way of being in the world that consternates on what isn't right or good, what could be better, or what could go away completely. The focus of this voice is on what is lacking. Why, oh why, are we so attached to focusing on what is wrong or bad, not right, and what is lacking?

Every recovery program asks the questions: "What have you lost that you are now ready to reclaim and recover?" This is a big question, which can truly bring one to realizing that there is more to getting clean and sober than just eliminating the substance or behavior of choice.

I know what I want – I want serenity! I want to come to accept what I cannot change. In essence, I want to recover my dignity, and know that place of peace within. I know it's there – I've experienced it dozens of time. There must be trick to getting it back and keeping it forever!

Yes, there is a trick – Yoda shares it in Star Wars: "Train yourself to let go of what you are afraid to lose." It's that simple. Oh, yeah, there's one other thing: stop doing what doesn't work, and what isn't in alignment with what it is you say you want. It's simple to say but challenging to sustain.

What makes this challenging is that our identity – which we believe ourselves to be - is attached to our perceptions, interpretations, and everything that is in our reality because of our perceptions and interpretations. We don't want to let go of what we are afraid to lose. It's scary as sh*t to experiment with who we are without our "stuffies" – my grandson's word for what makes him feel safe and secure with himself.

In general, what we are afraid to let go of is the belief that we are always in control; that we are not powerless, or helpless; and that the situation is not hopeless. Who are we – what are we - if we are not powerless, helpless and hopeless? That is the $50,000.00 dollar question.

Most of us are sissies, and aren't willing to engage the courage it would take to explore the edge of our comfort zones – just the edge of our comfort zone. The truth is, we never have to go outside of our comfort zones – we can empower ourselves to just expand our comfort zone one infinitesimal increment at a time. The internal space within each of us is the final frontier, and we've been trained not to go in there! We never ask "Why Not?"

It makes sense to me that for most individuals on this planet, we make the most progress regarding our spiritual development in the last two weeks of life. Why? Because, at this point, we see the inevitability and the futility of trying to prove that we are somebodies who are in control of their lives. We come to accept that we are powerless over the universal forces of LIFE, so we surrender our will. And, in doing so, we come to serenity and peace. AMEN!

When you look into the eyes of every individual with whom you come into contact, you will see a being who is challenged with malaise and fear, just as you are. We all struggle with "how can I get out of this alive?"

Aging like a guru means that you give yourself credit for being in the skin you are in. Love the one you are with – yourself. Give up the worries and frets of this specific moment and give yourself some fun – whatever that means to you! And rather than focusing on what is lacking in this moment, aging like a guru allows you to take on the practice of seeing what you do have, what is good, lovely, and what brings you joy – at whatever level.

John Lennon would say: "All I am saying is, give peace a chance!" Monty Python would say: "Always look on the bright side of life!" I, Dr. Rosie, would say: "Have all the fun you are willing to have – and more if possible!"

Chapter 6

Sit Back and Relax – Ready for Takeoff

Some people get on a plane and head out to their destination, effortlessly surrendering control to their pilots. Others are in the throes of panic – terrified of being out of control. They are hyper-vigilant for that moment when the plane blows up or crashes. They await the moment of impact when powerless, hopeless, & helplessness consumes them. Fortunately, for most of us, when we fly that moment never comes, but that doesn't stop many of us from sitting in wait.

I used to be that person, when it comes to flying. I am that person now, when it comes to other aspects of life. You see, how we do one thing is how we do everything. Whether it's getting on a plane, starting our day, or getting into bed at night, each aspect of life can be viewed as facing the unknown. The uncertainty keeps many people up through the night, as the relinquishment of their lives to sleep is an unbearable feat.

I used to be terrified of, well, just about everything. Actually, the truth is, and this is very Freudian, that I saw every moment of life as a potential moment for dying. Even at five years old, as best I could, I avoided being alone, because I was certain that I would die if I were alone. I'd sneak into my sister's bed once she was asleep, or take my pillow into my parents' room and slide under their bed so they wouldn't step on me if they got up in the middle of the night. Of course, they knew I was there, but they never said a thing.

Over my lifetime, thousands of my life choices were made based on ensuring that I wouldn't be alone. This didn't necessarily ensure I was happy, but it did ensure that I wasn't going to be alone – my sole purpose in life for a very long time.

I know a lot of people in their 40's and 50's who have never lived alone.

They move from their parents' home to their home with a roommate or their new spouse. Divorce, separation, or death may have been the only options for extricating them from their patterns of living in fear of being alone.

You see, no matter where we are in the aging process, we carry the same patterns living within us, unless we realize how limiting and stultifying this can be, and begin to try something different.

During the time that I was terrified of flying, I read something that said fear of flying was a result of the belief that you could not be rescued by a Prince or Princess Charming. Somehow understanding this liberated me from my fear of flying. And, over time I became brave enough to fly fearlessly, live on my own, cross the Atlantic Ocean in a sailboat (not alone), and step into many other adventures that, had I stayed in my fear, I'd still be back firmly entrenched in avoiding what scares me – being alone. I would have even stayed in a deadening marriage, living a life that was safe- but not fun!

Most of us are afraid of living alone because we are afraid of dying alone. Truth is, most of us do die alone. Circumstances are such that that's just the way it is. And could it be otherwise? We live within a body – a vessel that only we inhabit – and nobody else can live within the experience each of us individually have. Each of us have unique experiences of life that cannot ever be duplicated. Even if we are surrounded by people at the moment of death, we are having a unique experience unto ourselves.

Aging, when looked at with consciousness and wisdom, gives us opportunities to notice the ways we have chosen to live our lives. We have chosen to either enhance those ways of being that perpetuates suffering, settling, and surviving, or those that allow us to thrive and grow, expanding our capacity to be with the adventures that life offers, from the moment we land on earth to the moment our spirit takes off for parts unknown.

Throughout life, there are moments when we are not in control, and no matter what, we cannot control the circumstances. What we can control is how we be within the circumstance. First date, first kiss, first success, first cataract surgery, first incontinence episode, first erectile failure, first conversation with Social Security regarding Medicare . . . Nothing can prepare us for all those moments when we have no choice but to surrender into the excitement and exhilaration of life's gifts, or we clench, tremble, and hold our breath with every possibility that things could go wrong.

Those of you reading this today have successfully arrived at this moment in your life. You have overcome tremendous challenges and potential failures. You can trust that you can trust yourself to steward you through any hairy-scary circumstance. You can never be alone when you trust that you can trust yourself to get yourself through this too!

To age like a guru, is to know that surrender doesn't mean giving up. Surrender means letting go of those fears that limit your ability to be present in this moment. Taking a deep breath, relaxing into yourself and allowing yourself to be present to each of life's adventures, one moment at a time can be thrilling!

Chapter 7

Discerning the Essence of One's Life

Fearless Freedom

Barbara Herschel was a long time Orcas Islander. She was a big-hearted activist and advocated for changes that made our community more viable in so many ways. She was a real gift.

At the age of 78, Barbara hired me as her Life Coach. Her husband Bill passed away, and after a long time of caregiving for him, she was ready to return to those activities that made her heart soar. She wanted to paint again – something she was passionate about, yet she just couldn't get around to it. My job was to get her on track with her painting.

It wasn't uncommon for Barbara to be distracted with any number of issues that in the moment seemed critical, but were really not. One of those issues was her health. She was always running off the Island to see one doctor, or healer, or nutritionist. She had a heart problem, a hearing problem, and like most people in their late 70's, she experienced those challenges that come with the deterioration of one's physical being. Barbara spent a lot of time worrying about what frightened her most – having a heart attack and dying alone.

You wouldn't think that pulling out a bunch of paints, a canvas, and some brushes would warrant hiring a life coach, and the four years that Barbara and I spent together never did culminate in one single painting. Our work culminated in something far more exquisite and valuable, however. Through the discernment of the essence of Barbara, in the midst of her life, as it was, as it is, and as it would be, she came to discover who she was beyond her fears.

The day before Barbara died, she had an experience of self-empowerment and self-reliance that she had been longing for all her life. She called me, leaving a message on my answering machine – "I DID IT!" I will never forget the joy in her voice as she shared with me that ecstatic moment. She was no longer afraid. She was free.

Barbara died the next day, alone, of a heart attack. And I have no doubt she was at peace.

Fierce Love

My client Sarah is 62. She is a resident of the Bay Area, and is about to become the president of a highly renowned national organization for businesswomen. Sarah hired me as a life coach to help her figure out what the heck her life was about, and what she really wanted to do with the rest of her life.

Like Barbara, Sarah gets distracted with stuff that keeps her from really discerning the essence of her life and her work. She gets mired in those assumed critical issues of her complex life. Fortunately, Sarah is committed enough to realizing her truth that she quit her work as a life coach, took a month away from her husband and home, and went on retreat at her family's ranch in Idaho. Sarah is stepping into the presidency role in June, and as much as she has resistance about taking this position, she knows there is something bigger than her that compels her to take the seat of leadership for this organization.

In our most current session, we focused on what was at the heart and soul of the two years to come. By mining the truth of this, Sarah would potentially lead in alignment with her highest desires, and make her greatest contribution to the members of the organization, and to the country as well. If she didn't discern the essence of this work for herself, she would flounder in disorganized, scattered factions of what she thought other people expected of her.

My primary question for Sarah was the same question that I had for Barbara Herschel: What is the culmination of your being in this life? When discerning the essence of one's life and one's life work, the answer is the same. For Barbara, the essence was Fearless Freedom. For Sarah, it is Fierce Love.

Aging like a guru, regardless of where you are in the aging process, calls for discerning the essence of your life, or the roles you play within life, which then helps tremendously to get a sense of trajectory of what this is all about, where this is all leading for you. When coming into that sweet spot of recognition and knowing without a doubt that this is the essence of me, this is the essence of my work, life feels easier, more relaxed, and allows more openness, joy, and fun.

I have no doubt that Barbara died in fearless freedom. And I have no doubt that Sarah's leadership will culminate in women of the world growing themselves and their businesses from, and into, Fierce Love. When the essence of one's being is discerned and acted upon, how could it be any other way?

Addendum:

Two weeks before taking on the role as president of the organization, Sarah resigned her post. Through deep discernment she realized that in her present state of being she would not be a positive contributor to this organization and the women it served. It took fierce love for herself to sincerely know her truth, and to act on it.

Chapter 8

The Older I Get, the Luckier I Feel

Standing at the left cash register in the Island Hardware Store on Orcas Island, glancing into the back of the store, you will read: "If You are Lucky Enough to Live on Orcas Island, You are Lucky Enough."

It only took me 12 years of visiting Island Hardware to actually see this huge sign that is discolored with age. It had been there a long time, but somehow I missed these wise words. They have had a profound effect on me, because, up until the moment that I read those words, I took being *lucky enough* for granted. I saw life as a struggle, and that no matter how good life was, I believed it could always be better. This affected my attitude and my moods. I'd be happier if only...

Throughout my childhood, my parents began every morning in the glassed-in sun porch, overlooking the beautiful Detroit River. They sat with each other, their coffee, the crossword puzzles, and in solitude, awaiting the awakening of their hungry brood of nine children. They immersed themselves in the beauty of the day, more often than not, before dawn. This was the only time in their overwhelmingly busy lives when they could be bathed in Nature's essence. Only the sounds of the ducks and geese quacking and honking, the lake freighters, and small wooden fishing boats, cracked the sound of silence.

When we kids would wake up and interrupt my parent's solitude, my dad would inevitably say, "Isn't this the most beautiful day ever?" Because every day looked the same to me, I believed my dad was just making stuff up to get us look out the window and see outside ourselves.

Being *lucky enough* is an interesting experience, regardless of what stage of aging we are in. Like, at six, losing my front teeth, I thought I looked hideous, but at the same time, the Tooth Fairy brought me some money!

I felt *lucky enough!*

When I finally had my first boyfriend, I felt lucky enough to have someone who liked me. At the same time, I lost my sense of self by always trying to be what he wanted me to be. This was a lifelong pattern, one which made me pretty unhappy for much of my life. I finally got lucky enough when I got wise to the fact that I, me, myself, can value who I am, no matter what, and no matter who is around me!

We feel lucky when we find a job and quit a job; marry our dream mate and divorce them. We feel lucky when we imagine the morning rush hour traffic somewhere else, as we easily drive to work, waving to cars as they pass on the road to Eastsound.

There is a saying about boats and horses, probably planes and other big investments, too, that the luckiest day is the day you bought your boat, horse, plane, and the day you sold it. There are a lot of people who are feeling *lucky enough* right now!

Living in a small community, where going to the store is a social event in itself, makes me feel *lucky enough*. The clerks and cashiers who have been doing the same job for years, smile and greet me with a heartfelt hello. They are part of a network of people with whom I can laugh and be myself. I have a connection. This makes me feel luckier than most.

Every morning now, like my parents, I sit with my coffee in the midst of the beauty of Nature. I read and I write for the first hour of my day - not before dawn - ever. I feel lucky that my brain functions and allows me to string words together in at least a coherent fashion. I feel lucky that arthritis hasn't kicked in, so my fingers are pain-free for now. I feel lucky that my trailer is warm and comfortable, and that my Island Goods coffee tastes exactly the way I want it to. And, in this phase of my aging process, I am able to access and utilize wisdom like I've never been able to before. This definitely makes me *lucky enough!*

After an hour of writing, when it's time to take my dog Gracie for a walk, my hips and back are stiff and achy, but as I walk down my lane, and the aches and stiffness subsides, I feel lucky enough to have such freedom to move about.

After six decades of believing I knew more, and was smarter than everyone else - especially my parents, I now have a perspective on life and myself that allows me to be more open to what makes life worth living. Even though I thought I was smarter, that didn't make me I happier. I now know that I only have to be smart enough to know that I'm lucky enough.

Aging like a guru allows us to see the circumstances of life as opportunities to practice being lucky. It takes a great deal of faith, courage, and strength to cultivate an orientation in reality that displays all the gifts of being lucky, yet it is very, very possible, indeed.

Chapter 9

Victim of Life's Circumstances . . . or Not!

Francis, a beautiful, creative woman and longtime Island resident, visited my workplace the other day. *"I've been reading your articles on aging and dying, in Orcas Issues, and you know,"* she said with a wee bit of disdain in her voice, *"Aging isn't all fun and light – sometimes there's anger and hate. I've been dealing with hearing loss for a long time. My memory is deteriorating and I'm afraid that I'm losing my mind. I'm living with a lot of pain. I'm alone more often than not, and I'm angry about all of this. Sometimes I hate being alive. I just wanted you to know that!* "

About 8 years ago, some friends of mine, Harvey and Kate, while sitting at a stoplight in their cute little sports car, having a beautiful peaceful day off Island, were struck from behind by a very big truck. It crushed the easy-going brilliant life that they knew was theirs. Physical injury and trauma to the brain completely changed their orientation to life. The degree to which they have recovered allows a great deal of mobility and possibilities; however, every day they live with the consequences of their life choices. They live with chronic pain and an inability to rely on their mental capabilities; they live with their choice to buy a little sports car, drive off Island that fateful day, and to choose within every moment of life how they will face the unknown that arises every day.

For decades, my friend Marvin worked for the airlines until he retired. Every day, as he loaded and unloaded baggage from airplanes, he was exposed to the sound of those jet engines that can blind a person with sound. Marvin suffers with major hearing loss because of his choice of jobs. He too, like Francis, Harvey and Kate, at times, questions the choices he made and the consequence of those choices.

Personally, I've yet to be affected by the 3 D's of aging: Decline, Depletion and Deterioration like Frances has; nor have I been affected by other life circumstances such as Marvin, Harvey and Kate, that could not be anything other than annihilating to one's frame of reference. I also have all my faculties - the ones that I rely on to navigate reality and allow me to be in relationship with the world & communities within which I exist: my sight, hearing, mobility, & mental faculties.

I didn't go to war, where one loses limbs, friends, and too often peace of mind. I did however choose marriage, parenthood, divorce, and separation from my children. To choose this and not something else required me to deal with the ravages of the death of innocence, and the loss of hope that love will prevail.

Life's battles, regardless of how mundane they appear to be, require each of us to accept what is, which can be as horrendous and traumatic as anything imaginable.

I don't know of a single person who has lived a life free of some form of trauma due to choices they have made, or that were made by others. Each of us are left to our own devices to be with the consequences of those unforeseen, undesired events. Essentially, we either choose to frame our reality in the perspective of victimhood, or we choose to see the bigger picture: one that lies beyond powerlessness, hopelessness, and helplessness.

Truly, no one likes this particular conversation I'm having with you through this writing, even though it circles around in our mental conversations continuously. We experience the hardships of our circumstances, while at the same time we courageously muster the strength to live within the consequences of life's undoing. It seems impossible and unrealistic to even attempt to shift our frame of reference from seeing ourselves as victims of decline, deterioration, and depletion of life force, to a perspective which provides opportunities to experience who we are as our essential selves, within these difficult and undesired experiences.

I Now Know Who I Am

It is because of those unanticipated, unwanted, despicable life circumstance that I've come to experience who I am in the truest sense. If I hadn't been forced into certain circumstances that stretched my capacity to question reality, question faith, question truth, then I wouldn't have grown my ability to even experience serenity. I couldn't have experienced first-hand how grace works in such profound ways. I wouldn't have developed the tools to empower others to find their ways to serenity through grace.

Truth is, most of us live with our circumstances, frustrated, disappointed, angry and sometimes hateful. We don't have a way of seeing it any other way. So we avoid and distract ourselves from our agony and our fears, hoping that someday there will be ease, grace, and serenity.

I believe that whatever circumstance we currently sit in, regardless of age, race, religion, gender, sexual preference, or political orientation, we each reach a moment where we examine who we are within our life choices, our life circumstances. We rail and flail against forces that have brought us to this moment. We resist grieving the loss of the world we once knew, experienced, and hoped would always be.

We hate those who ignore our plight, those who won't even try to accept us as we are now, with all of our failings and faults. We feel marginalized, isolated, cast out, useless, without purpose, and most importantly, without a true knowing of Self that guides and companions each of us through life's unfolding.

Aging like a guru allows each individual to recognize that choice-point where they can choose to surrender all of that – all of the suffering created by using the compass of discontent. They recognize this point in time, this moment, as an opportunity to admit that they are powerless, perhaps even helpless, and that their situation is hopeless. None of us truly look forward to this moment of choice. Few of us actually choose a path of acceptance, and fully allow the joy that is accessible through acceptance.

This isn't heartbreaking news, because every one of us has the ability to age like a guru and to choose the life worth living. Except for a very few, every one of us has the ability to let go of what no longer serves a life of serenity. I smile as I write this, because I know that the possibility for each of us to create that joy is so very near.

Chapter 10

The Well Worn Path of Anticipation

As a child, my focus of attention was quite often on the future. I anticipated the delight of holidays – Thanksgiving, Christmas, and the 4th of July, to name a few. I anxiously awaited the time when I was old enough to go to church, or begin school – being like the big kids in my family. I longed for my first crush, my first date, my first kiss, and my first, well, you know!

I couldn't wait until I could leave my parents' home, go off to college, find a husband, get married and have children. Then with the unhappiness of my marriage, I longed for and anticipated the way out of this marriage. Once out, I anticipated my next big relationship, finishing graduate school, getting a job as a therapist.... So much of my life was lived in anticipation.

Living Life in a Constant State of Anticipation

Living life in a constant state of anticipation has been a recurring theme in our Tuesday discussion group "Aging-Who Me?" This past week, John says, "All my life I've lived in anticipation – always looking forward to the next terrific adventure. Now that I'm old, my anticipations are a lot smaller in scope, like anticipating my morning visit to the post office and to Teasers for coffee. These are as fulfilling today as the more fantastical adventures of my past."

The others in the room nod their heads, acknowledging John and what he is sharing. Margaret says she has noticed that what used to get her out of bed in the morning – what she anticipated and compelled her to jump out of bed - doesn't exist anymore. There are fewer and fewer things that excite her enough to leave the comforts of her bed, so she lingers until something gets her up.

I asked the question of the group: "We live so much of our lives in the state of anticipation – where would we be if we weren't in anticipation?" Lorraine shouts out, "In the now!" Everyone nods their head and joins Loraine in this idea that, if we aren't living in anticipation, then we are living in the present moment. There is a pregnant pause. Then the question that begs to be asked is: "What is it that has us choose to spend so much of our lives anticipating the future? And, what are we missing out on in the present while we are always busy mentally creating our future?"

Ellen adds, "Yes, and it isn't that we are just anticipating positive things happening. A lot of my time is anticipating the not so good things happening. Worrying is a form of anticipation too, right?"

So in our anticipation of the good and the bad things occurring, we are not attending to who we are and what is occurring in the here and now. Many of us don't even know how to do this. How many of us carry our cell phones anticipating the next text, email, or Facebook notification? I find this fascinating.

I wrote a book about 8 years ago called The Unholy Path of a Reluctant Adventurer. It is a recalling of my life lived between the life I anticipated and the life I actually lived. I anticipated my whole life being content as a mom, wife, and just a part of the community on Niagara Falls, Ontario. I never anticipated leaving my children in the custody of their dad, living in Nova Scotia, crossing the Atlantic Ocean, or getting numerous graduate degrees, including a PhD. I also never anticipated writing books, or living on Orcas Island. I never anticipated that I'd be thoroughly enjoying living in a travel trailer for 13 years. I just didn't see any of this coming!

Somewhere between that state of anticipation and the state of being in the present moment, there must be another state of being – perhaps that meta-state I speak about in the chapter "Game Changers – They Happen When Least Expected." But in this state that appears to be between anticipation and living in the now, life is unfolding. I believe it is the road less traveled. It is available to us all, but few willingly explore such territory.

To age like a guru, I believe we have more access to this state of being. With less stamina and energy, we begin to be more selective of what we wish to bring into our lives. As we age, most people say they want more peace and less angst; so they choose accordingly. The anticipation of just opening their eyes and seeing the light of day can bring as much excitement as a child waking up on Christmas Day. It is a challenging practice to anticipate the now, however I believe that aging like a guru provides us with the wisdom to take on this practice effortlessly.

Chapter 11

Will I like This When I'm Done?

I'm just coming back to the Island after participating in a Kuhn Sisters' Week in Michigan. I had a lot of trepidation in setting out to attend this event – will I like this when I'm done? I decided to head out anyway, thinking about it as an adventure, with no expectations. Just go!

My four sisters and I love to create art and crafts. So, one part of our time together was Craft Day, when we would all sit around the table making something fun and beautiful. On a hot and humid Michigan day, it creates a time for more personal connections and conversations to emerge. And, the bonus? We each take home a little memento of our time together.

The excitement of beginning – the moment a project is started, whether it's knitting, painting, golf, parenting, or stepping into a new phase of life, you never know what you'll have in the end. You might like it, you might hate it. The only way you will find out is to just start.

My sister Helene and I chose a beautiful shawl pattern, one that my sister Annie finished recently.

Neither of us have knitted in a long time, but we dove in, excited about the possibility of loving the outcome. We loved the yarn and pattern, but would we love it when we're done?

Helene, who hasn't knitted for decades, feels the angst of beginning. "I can't do it!" she exclaims, even though she hasn't even tried. I observe her flitting about the house, being distracted by any number of things, unable to stay in this new practice of knitting. It is only a matter of eight new stitches to learn and implement, row after row, but it is daunting to her nevertheless.

I jump in, having Annie as my knitting coach. I feel an ease with the process, and it really helps when I see Annie making the occasional mistake, ripping it out, and studying the pattern – it's the roadmap to her final destination. Like all travelers on any of the myriad of roads of creativity, you have to be willing to see where you are and where you have been. When lost, you go back to where you knew yourself to be, assess the situation, study the map, and start out again. You might have to return again and again to this point, but it's very comforting to know that this point exists!

As a master at creativity – quilts, paintings, knitting, life - Annie accepts that sometimes, when lost and unsure where she is in the process, she too has to stop. On many occasions, she will rip the piece apart, until she gets to that place where she knows where she is. Sometimes, she just rips it all out and starts all over again. She too never knows if she's going to like her creation, but onward she treads. She says, "If I hate it, I'll just take it apart and make something different, or I'll just give it to the Salvation Army." Lucky Salvation Army, is what I say!

Patrice is also an amazing craft person and life voyager. She has a lot of practice embarking on new projects and seeing them through to the end. Less than 10 months ago, Patrice, at 66 years of age, began making a new relationship with her sweetie, David. She isn't worrying about whether she's going to like it when she's done. She is thoroughly engaged in being present and focused on each individual stitch of love she makes, creating a pattern of happiness for her and her beloved.

Making relationships as an art form is challenging. Two people are required to bring about the fulfillment of the project. Every day, Patrice and David weave together the threads of their thoughts, feelings, their desires and hopes. The unfolding tapestry is something unique to each and every couple. They do not have a pattern or road map that they are following. In these precious moments, their hearts know the destination. And, right now, they are in complete certainty that they will love it when they are done.

. . . .

Annie texts me on her layover in LAX. "I'm frustrated! I'm not as far home as I want to be!" Impatience is the teacher of humility and acceptance. It's funny how often we want to get to the end and bypass the hard parts. We want to be in that place where we cruise through life, or our crafts, and know with certainty we will like what we've created. No one likes the hard parts, except those who are masochists, and those who truly know that the wisdom of life and love emerges through being with the hard stuff.

Speaking of hard stuff, my sister Mary Therese is also starting something new. After two years of living with stage four ovarian cancer, she is at the beginning of the end, again. There isn't much more the doctors can do for her. She says, "I'm afraid I'm not going to like this when I'm done!"

There are aspects of life that allow us to live in the hopes that we will like what we've created. Facing death as our final project, well, none of us are practiced at dying – we won't know if we like it until it's done. We can't tear out our mistakes and start over. No do-overs!

Aging like a guru means knowing that every part of life, just like every project and hobby we engage in, brings us to these moments where we hope we are going to like it when we are done, but not sure how it's going to end. We fear for the worst and hope for the best. For each of us, though, there is that certain something that spurs us on to finish what we start. One's life is no exception.

Chapter 12

Game Changers - They Happen When Least Expected

Sam is a 73-year-old retired fellow, living in a two-bedroom apartment in Houston. He is a veteran from the Viet Nam era, had a decent enough life with a couple of kids, an ex-wife, and a girlfriend of 25 years. Sam has been happy in his routines – stopping in at his local bank where he has coffee with some cronies. He visits with neighbors and participates in his community, as he has done for many decades.

A longtime client of mine, James, in his mid 40's, lives in Denver. He has four children, a wife he adores, a business that in this moment is supporting the family, and he has been sober for almost 20 years. James calls me because he feels he is about to fall off the wagon. He doesn't know what to do!

James got a call from his dad's girlfriend a few months back. She said that Sam's memory is going. He can't live alone anymore. She told James to come get his father and take him back to Denver.

After three months of Sam living in the basement of his home, James is caught in the Big Fat Be-With of his father's failing memory plus the financial fiascos of a person with no will and no plans for this part of his life. They are dealing with the VA, Elderly Day Care centers, and long-term care facilities. Yesterday they got the diagnosis that it is most likely Alzheimer's. None of this was part of their reality until they got the call three months ago.

Sam wants to go home – back to his apartment and to his routines in Houston. He is angry, isolated, lonely, confused, and trapped in his son's world. Sam and James are living in different realities. James pleads with me, "Rosie, just tell me what to do!"

I rarely tell people what to do. Why? Because rarely are people willing to practice what I preach. However, I give James some instructions. "First, James, educate yourself on dementia and Alzheimer's. Google any and every question you have. Utilize the experience and knowledge of the millions of people who have gone through what you are currently going through." Then there is *the pause* that tells me he isn't going to do what I instructed him to do. I ask, "What's happening right now, James?"

James begins to share how he doesn't have time to educate himself about his father's illness; that he needs to attend to his roofing business, which is lacking his attention, as is his wife, family, and his own health. I totally get it, and, so do millions of families that find themselves in James' shoes – with an unexpected circumstance – an uninvited intrusion on an already overwhelming life. It is crazy-making in every way possible. And, there is no way out!

This week, James is flying to Houston to close out his father's apartment. He will bring back to Denver a few remnants of Sam's life. He doesn't want to do this. He doesn't want to be responsible for doing all the things that need to be done. He doesn't want one more thing to get in the way of trying to live the life he thinks he should be living. He doesn't want to admit that he is actually a grownup who now has to find a way to make challenging choices for a person that doesn't want his help.

I ask James: "What if this is as good as it gets?" James responds: "Rosie, this is as good as it gets, and I don't like it one bit!" I ask the question all of my clients hate: "James, since this, then, is as good as it gets, what is it like inside you, in the midst of all this ever-increasing turmoil?"

James answers: "I feel powerless. And, I don't like feeling powerless. I feel like I'm stepping off a cliff into the abyssness of not knowing. There is no sanity, reason, or helpfulness in this place. But here I am!" Now we are getting somewhere!

No person that I know looks forward to when they are the caregiver for a family member who is failing mentally, physically, or spiritually for that matter. Few prepare themselves for disease, decline and death of parents, partners or children. Most people I know fear the moment when they are asked to put their life on hold in order to support others in a way they never thought about before. They are asked to choose between what they believed to be their highest priority – quite often money, and what wasn't even close to the top of the list – the care and nurturing of a person who may not know who they are anymore. Yes, Sam is beginning to forget that James is his son.

The process of aging has caught James off-guard, yet when he and I talked a second time this week he was more centered and grounded. Where earlier in the week he was split and pulled in many directions, today he knows that is he is on his true path, at least in this moment. In this moment of clarity he can see that he is immersed in an experience that he knows will change his life in a good way.

Stephen Levine, who is a very wise person, said something like, *diseases, such as cancer and Alzheimer's, are gifts for the person who has everything*. That statement packs a wallop of wisdom. When we are immersed in the material world, we often lose connection with the world of the meta-physical; the meta-world that is the driving force of what is desired and manifested in the material world. It's our thoughts, emotions and body sensations. And, it is the intelligence of all of life.

When we find ourselves in a game-changing situation, we are usually required to question reality. When we question reality we find ourselves sometimes powerless within the material world, yet curiously empowered to be present to the meta-world – thoughts, emotions, body sensations, intuitions, Divine guidance, and more. With access to this part of life, one can choose based on a deeper sense of truth and a deeper knowing of self. James is exploring his meta-world for a foundation upon which to respond to what life is currently demanding of him.

This is all a kick-in-the-head for James and his family. They are beginning to reorient values and priorities to align with their desire to care for Sam in the most humane and loving way possible. As James reflects on his circumstances, he is beginning to appreciate those values that were long ignored, though he knew they were far more important than he wanted to admit.

Aging like a guru means maturing, wising-up, expanding one's orientation to the world, discovering a personal way of looking at life that allows grace and dignity to exist within everyone. This family – Sam, James, and the rest - are accepting the invitation to age, mature, and to wise-up in the most loving way possible, through the game-changers that were least expected. What a gift!

Chapter 13

Your Life is a Testimony to Change

The more years I have under my belt, the more I realize the degree to which life is more about change than it is about no-change. That change occurs in the realms of physical, mental, and emotional development; social and political structures; career and finances; relationships with family and community; and last but not least, relationships with ourselves and our spirituality. How could one possibly interpret life as stable with all of the shifts that occur in so many aspects of one's reality?!

In the past, I believed if I earned enough Merit Badges in my life, harm and suffering would remain at bay. I believed that if I think the right thoughts, be charitable, and try to do no harm to myself and others, I'd be allowed to avoid the hairy-scary, life-shattering episodes that no one wants to experience.

As I age, more and more often, wisdom sheds light on predicaments and circumstances in ways that allow me to see that to a huge degree, I'm not in control of whether I get sick, whether I'm impoverished financially, whether I am homeless, whether my relationships are all happy and loving, or whether my career path is smooth. I've learned to let go of my assumptions and expectations that life is going to go my way, especially if I try really hard to "will" it to be my way.

As I age, I find that what I thought life was about is not what life is about. It's about something else entirely. If you are anything like me, you've worked hard to have the right stuff, as in having the right education, the right career, the right spouse and children, the right home, the right 401K, stock portfolio and other investments to ensure you are right where you want to be when you want to be there.

I'm exhausted thinking about what it takes to accumulate and manage the accumulation. But, this is what life is about – right? Or, this is what life should be about – right?

For some people, it's about rejecting all of this, fighting for liberty from the evils of stuff. These individuals spend their lives judging and criticizing people who put all their efforts into accumulating stuff. They resist being part of consensus reality, and experience a righteous indignation because they believe they are outside the norm.

I'm exhausted thinking about all of the resistance required to attempt to control life. It might be time for a nap!

Who are we when we are not accumulating and not resisting accumulation? Who are we when we aren't fighting to control our weight, our health, our portfolio, our partners and children? Who are we when we relinquish the fight for an identity or role that is deemed important and valued by others? Who are we?

As we age, many of us are forced to let go of what we've accumulated over our lifetimes: we downsize our careers, our houses, families. We discover that putting effort into anything that isn't fun is actually exhausting. We become more vigilant about what brings joy. We discover simplicity is much more enjoyable. Sitting outside, watching a tree grow becomes an experience of wonder and delight – an experience that captivates one's humanness and is soul-fulfilling.

When I was in my early 20's and just beginning to cultivate accumulations: husband, house, stuff, I had a next-door neighbor named Reg. Reg was an old, retired Welsh fellow. Most of the time he sat in his backyard for hours every day and watched the seasons change.

Reg had an enormous Chestnut Tree in his backyard. Squirrels and birds populated that tree and entertained Reg all day long. He would come out after breakfast, go in for lunch, which his wife Ann had fixed him, then come out in the afternoon until the sun went down.

I'd often go and visit ol' Reg. I felt sorry for him. I thought his life must be boring, and because he had angina, he had to stay relatively quiet. That is how I saw ol' Reg.

One day, Reg's wife died unexpectedly. Reg still sat outside with his tree.

Then one day, because the tree was dying, and branches were beginning to precariously fall on neighbors' gardens, the tree was cut down and taken away. I experienced it as an amputation of a part of Reg's being. I believe that losing this tree, this constant companion, was when Reg really began to die. His children sold the house and Reg disappeared from my life forever. Well, sort of.

Forty-five years after meeting Reg, he is still very much a part of my life – in fact, I'm a lot like Reg. Where at first I interpreted Reg as being bored and having nothing better to do, I came to see that truly there was nothing better to do. The simplicity of Reg's world was perfect. Sitting outside, watching the unfolding of Spring, Summer, Fall and Winter brings me huge delight, as it did Reg. The exquisiteness of even one single bird flitting across the yard makes my heart soar.

Aging like a guru means believing that life is a fascinating process for each individual on the planet. If we are lucky enough to get to the age when we are considered old, we begin to participate in the unfolding process of the being within. We see that there is a ME within that isn't affected by how much or how little one has; a ME that doesn't care so much about vanity of any sort – beauty yes, vanity not so much.

Aging like a guru allows one to consciously experience an evolution of Self, whether we acknowledge it or not. If we are here long enough, inside our human suit, we begin to value that which we've been attempting to value all along: Life, as in the acknowledgment and the honoring of the being within all of life – no exceptions.

Change is a constant in everyone's life, yet change is what we fear most, because with change comes loss. And, though we so wish to avoid loss and grief, there is no way to avoid the inevitable unfolding of what comes and what goes. I believe that as we age (hopefully like gurus!), we are gifted with a multitude of opportunities to shift our expectations and arrive in the serenity of acceptance and allowance.

The adventures of aging are gifts that are given to those who are curious enough to stick around. Curiosity builds courage and resilience, and change becomes the part of life that makes it a great page-turner – you just can't wait to see what's gonna happen in the next chapter.

Chapter 14
Aging – the Unfolding Perfection

Most of us on Orcas Island love our flowers. After our cold and wet, rainy winters, the dreariness can do nothing but encourage hope for spring to come ASAP! When leaf and flower buds begin to emerge, our hearts well up with delight. We see the world as burgeoning perfection. All is good with the world.

Intrinsic beauty exists as much in the anticipation within our ecstatic hearts as it does in the bud itself. I have a Dogwood tree that brings me such joy. Every moment of its life cycle evokes sensations of rapture within me. It is a dance we do together. It is a dance I welcome into my life.

On the other hand, my body, over the years, has been unfolding through its own life cycle, always in a complete state of perfection, regardless of how I have chosen to judge that perfection. In my youth I wanted to grow into my fully mature self as quickly as possible. I was frustrated that I couldn't hurry it up. I wanted to experience the sensations of a first kiss. I wanted to know what falling in love felt like. I wanted to know how it felt to experience a tiny growing baby within my belly as it move and kicked, and the experience of the bonding that takes place while nursing my babies at my breast.

When I blossomed into the woman I was, I was never satisfied. I worked at being fit because I wanted to look perfect and be perfect in my own mind. I imagined that I had the rest of my life to perfect me. I was right in some respects and not so right in others.

I remember some of the first signs of aging – the one that told me I was now officially in the "declining years." One such moment was when I was 47 years old, and I saw that my skin was becoming crepe-like. At that moment, the bloom was off the rose for me – no pun intended.

Like so many people I speak to about aging, I too avoid looking in the mirror. When I see my reflection, what is looking back at me is not who I expect to see. Wrinkles, bags, sags, plumbs, with a little slouch for an added touch, glare back at me. I shut my eyes so as to pretend I can deny that I'm not the young one anymore. Why is it that we don't relish every wrinkle, every laugh line, every grey hair, every nuance of the humanness that this body – this being - is experiencing? Why do we beat ourselves up? Why do we degrade the exceptional human experience that is occurring for the entirety of one's life? We are such silly beings!

Since I've begun writing this book and working part time in the Box Office at Orcas Center, where I talk with aging people all the time, I've shifted in the way that I experience people – especially those I could consider old, not young. This begs the question – at least for me: *Well, what were you experiencing before this shift, and, what actually shifted?*

Before the shift, I experienced fear when I looked at aging people. I feared their differences. I feared the discomfort within me when I was in their presence. I feared the humiliation when I wouldn't know how to talk with them in a respectful and kind way. I feared that my ignorance of the life of the elderly would have them feel isolated, ignored, and unappreciated. I saw through the lens of imperfections, judgments; I was critical of every visible limitation. No wonder going to Senior Lunch was so difficult: before the shift, I witnessed an environment of decline. The discomfort was unbearable. And it was only a reflection of my belief of what I would be evolving into.

Through the *Aging-Who Me?* discussions at the Senior Center, through this book, and through assisting people at the Box Office, the shifts that occurred have brought more reverence and compassion for all people. Like looking at a flower, regardless of its phase of life, I see the essential beauty and perfection that is within each individual. Where I used to assess and judge people in a matter of a nano-second, I now absorb the radiant beauty of who stands before me, or who is on the other end of the phone line.

Sometimes, I'm not so good at this. But I believe that the most valuable aspect of this shift I'm speaking of is that I have become much more aware of what drives my negative reactions to people in the world, and, I can catch myself more often than not when I experience within me that critical judge. I no longer enjoy feeling that feeling of judginess.

I willingly desire and discipline myself to see everyone in the beauty of their essential nature. I like that feeling better.

The Illusion of Moving from Perfect to Imperfect

Depending on the culture within which each of us has been raised, to one degree or another, we have learned to dismiss the elderly. And, those who are experiencing that dismissal are getting younger and younger – the corporate environment these days view people in their 40's as over the hill and all washed up. The cosmetic companies make trillions of dollars training us to view the natural and beautiful aging process as a horrible affliction. We have learned to interpret every aspect of our being, whether we are men or women, not as perfectly perfect, but as embarrassing and humiliating. It is really sad, isn't it?

The truth is, aging like a guru allows us to be more at choice to view the world through lenses that allow us to experience perfection evolving into perfection. It's really not that hard, and it is actually an outrageously exquisite experience! Try it, you'll like it!

Chapter 15

Old Dogs Do Learn New Tricks

My dog Gracie is almost eight years old. She has been chasing frisbees her whole life. But it was just last week that she actually caught one on the fly. I could see her mind working that day, working out the mechanics, figuring out the potential trajectory of my throw, and as she was running, she looked over her left shoulder and saw the frisbee coming. She leaped into the air and caught it! It was a glorious moment for Gracie, one she wanted to repeat, again and again!

My friend Lorna, who is 72, in human years, brought herself to an orgasm – the first time in her life. Though her relationship with her partner Craig is still hot after 35 years, Lorna had never been able to pleasure herself to orgasm until this fateful day. It was a glorious moment for Lorna – one she wants to repeat again and again.

People think of me as an academic because of the many graduate degrees that are part of my history. Actually I'm a learner, definitely not an academic. Academia has been a path for learning, but really, life itself has been the greatest institution of higher learning available – that and YouTube.

Learning is a life-changing phenomenon. Every time you learn something new, a paradigm shift occurs and your reality is stirred, perhaps even shaken.

Learning is the ineffable connection of ourselves with universal wisdom. You may think I'm going too far out there, however, it isn't just the accumulation of knowledge that we seek. There is something else. When we learn something new, or even try to learn something new, we touch into the potential of reality every time. Yes, the potential of reality, as well as the reality of potential. How exciting is that?

I've witnessed revelations in people at all ends of the spectrum of aging: Carl, who is learning to walk without pain, after his hip surgery, and my grandson Andrew as he picked up a wooly caterpillar for the very first time. Both were struck with wonder, and delight shone on both of their faces.

From the beginning of our time on Earth, learning brings us understanding of who we are and what our function is in this world. We learn to assume many roles and identities. As we grow, quite often we attend to the accomplishment, while disconnected from the Being who is inside all of the learning, functioning, and developing.

In the midst of learning, we have an opportunity to experience ourselves within the moment of transcendence, when we take that leap of faith. I see this in my friend Marj: when in the midst of experimenting with her acrylic painting something unexpected happens, and audible sounds of delight spontaneously erupt. By experimenting and practicing different ways of thinking, different ways of seeing, and different ways of moving in the world, light bulbs go on, and we feel a little more connected to our selves. Deep, right?

Aging like a guru is to immerse ourselves in learning opportunities and relish the experience of uncovering and experiencing the learner within the learning. To age like a guru takes focused dedication and discipline. Every day, as the aging process becomes more self-evident, it requires constant vigilance and openness to learning who we are in this moment. What works now? What doesn't work any longer?

Just like learning to play a musical instrument, or learning to ride a bike, it requires a constant presence to what is now. It's letting go of habits, identities, and patterns that worked in the past but now limit our capacity to thrive and enjoy life. Marj let go of some rigidity in her body that allowed a flow to happen on her canvas. Lorna let go of decades of patternings to allow her to release into what had been forbidden her whole life.

Learning like a guru requires making mistakes. Making mistakes allows us to connect to our humanness and fallibility. Our fallibility leads us to humility, no longer humiliation and embarrassment. As we mature, we realize that the fear of making mistakes is highly overrated. Carl shared with me that because he feared making the wrong decision about getting his hip replaced he missed out on a lot of fun. He isn't going to make that mistake again. "I want the fun!" he said, "And, I'm going to do whatever it takes to make sure I stay in this mindset."

Throughout life we cultivate competencies. And the popular presumption is that, as we age, we lose those competencies. This quite often scares most of us into playing safe, and limiting opportunities to get hurt. We then participate only in activities, mental and physical, that assist us in ignoring and avoiding the reality that we don't seem to have that resilience we once had. Carl was headed in that direction and turned himself around. You go, Carl!

In our Tuesday morning discussion group, *Aging* – Who Me? one wise woman presented the idea that, perhaps there is a gift in learning to let go of what no longer works. Maybe through the practice of letting go we learn to look at ourselves and our lives differently. Maybe this aging process, especially within this phase which seems to demand so much of us in accepting what we cannot change, we learn to be curious about who is inside these bags of bones. Through curiosity we discover things about ourselves we never even knew existed, though have always been in there.

The process of aging like a guru requires learning something new every day, if only in service to figuring out how to get out of bed, how to hold your pee, how to work around arthritis, how to remember to take which pills at the correct time. My hope for us all is that we revel in the delight of every accomplishment – no matter how small. It's the experience of reveling, not the accomplishment, that is the true gift. Every day, we old dogs really are learning new tricks.

Chapter 16

Nobody Does It like Mother Nature

I've heard it said that death is the great equalizer. As true as this statement is, I see that aging too is the great equalizer. Stuff happens as we age, and no matter how much power, money, beauty, or sex-appeal you have, you can't say no to what Mother Nature has to offer.

One of the intentions of this book, *Aging Like a Guru,* is to cultivate not only awareness but also our innate intelligence in a way that sparks a curiosity about what it is like within these human packages. Another intention is to see that, regardless of your chronological age, you are most likely always in the question: *Aging – Who Me?!*

Can you remember the first time that you thought about death? (I was 5.) Can you remember the first sign of aging that you noticed on or in your body? (I was 35.) I suspect that from that moment on, you became vigilant, if not hyper-vigilant to any and all follow-up indications that aging was happening to you.

Sex appeal, money, and power can only go so far. DENIAL can only work for so long. Substances such as alcohol, anti-depressants, and anti-anxiety medications, facelifts, and the rest, only allow us to avoid and numb the human experience within the aging process that is occurring to us. At some point, relentless vanity must succumb to reality. Humiliation dies a hard death, out of which sweet humility is born. Such is the gift from Mother Nature.

I love how when talking with people in their 60's, 70's, 80's or 90's, they express that they don't feel old inside – they feel like they are in their 30's or younger. They still feel like a kid, and desire and enjoy all the pleasures that were part of their younger lives – that never goes away.

So, at some point we can distinguish ourselves from the sack of bones that for decades we believed was us. And, we can come to discover that we aren't aging, it is our bodies that are aging. We get wise, enough to be able to handle the truth of this fact, and willingly detach our identity from our bodies. We wise up and realize that there is no point in fighting Mother Nature. This doesn't mean we get depressed and crawl into our graves before our time. No. No. No. It actually means just the opposite!

Aging like a guru means that there are many points in life where we choose to detach ourselves from who we thought we were, who we wished we were, and who we pretended to be. We come to surrender and accept that this Life-Journey provides many opportunities to question the purpose of being on this planet. All of the physical signs of aging – a big package of humility-building opportunities, wrapped in a big bow, are a gift from Mother Nature for those who dare to ask again and again and again: *who am I, what's the point of my presence on this planet, and, how will I know when I'm done?*

Each of us, as aging gurus, has our own unique answers to these questions. I've discovered that many people, including myself, who willingly sit with themselves and with these questions, are most likely to discover a lightness of being within. We smile more, even laugh, though the circumstances of aging will inevitably put us in our graves. We come to know ourselves as the ageless one within. We come to accept that we are not our circumstances – we aren't even our wrinkly, old bodies. As aging gurus we stop taking the whole life-thing so seriously, and come to enjoy the simpler pleasures of just being.

Regardless of our age, each of us face a plethora of choice-points that challenge our sense of Self. Though grueling and difficult, each life choice prepared us and has led us to this moment of truth, this moment of courage in facing the inevitability that we won't make it out of this alive. Now what? You have to see the humor in that! Or, maybe not yet!!

Just for grins, here is a video of singer Stan Boreson, singing "You Just Don't Look Good Naked Anymore." https://youtu.be/3_6I50oXAVM

Chapter 17

Ageism Among the Aged – That's Wacky!

I know plenty of individuals in their 60's, 70's and 80's who don't want to hang around with "old people." These old people may be the same age, yet, they are seen as different, because they are seen as old. Isn't that fascinating. When is Old Old, and what is Old, anyway?

Orcas Island Senior Lunch

The room is a sea of white-haired people, sitting around tables, apparently enjoying the company of others. Quite often a piano player is providing beautiful and joyful music. To some, this is very inviting!

Depending on which table you visit, you may find people talking about the domino game that will follow lunch. At another table they are talking about aches and pains, body part replacements, or how so-and-so just got medi-vac'd off the island. At another table, there is talk about singing at the next talent show; another, about visiting children and grandchildren. There is a table of individuals talking politics, about good books, or the upcoming live-streaming of an opera or ballet. And at another, they are talking sports, hunting, and fishing. You just never know.

When you walk into the room, based on what you think and believe about aging, you may not see yourself as one of them, one of those white-haired people. In that moment, you may be thinking: *I'm not one of them – I'm not aging and I'm not getting old.*

Somehow, we don't see that, aside from being a white-haired person, there are a lot of amazingly creative and brilliant people sitting in the midst of that snowy white hair. What we see is what we view through the lens of our personally-cultivated and highly-valued interpretations about old people. We humans are such fascinating beings. We create all sorts of thoughts and impose them on the world we live in.

This chapter isn't about promoting the Senior Center, because there are a lot of people who aren't interested in the social aspect of the Center. This chapter is about how so many of us look at ourselves as separate and different, and how we may alienate others, even though they are just like us. This may be just too scary to accept!

Ageism, like Racism, Sexism, Classism, or any other -ism, is based on beliefs, judgments, and assessments that quite often have nothing to do with the truth. All ISMs involve a negative prejudgment, whose purpose is to maintain the sense of power and control within ourselves. In the Recovery Community, any ISM stands for Inner Sh*t Maintained. Ouch! That hits home!

The other night, I had an interesting experience that serves this point. While brushing my teeth, I notice that my gums are receding. The term "Long in the Tooth" came up, and I was instantaneously triggered. This gum receding thing is just another indication that I am, indeed, getting old.

I climbed into bed, and because I'm not only writing this book on aging and change, but also leading discussions on aging at the Senior Center, I kind of had to be with this experience with a little bit more attention. Sure, the receding gums could be caused by something other than aging, but in this moment, aging is what got triggered.

By allowing myself to be with what was happening, I experienced what felt like an eruption of emotion, like lancing a boil or a cyst. (Gross, I know!) Though highly uncomfortable, I had to be with all of what showed up.

Primarily, I experienced much of what I believe is just part and parcel of being human. The bottom line – in that moment – is that I experienced myself as a complete and utter failure; that this life and all its efforts has culminated into nothing. Deep humiliation arose, as did the "truth:" my life had no meaning and no value.

This all occurred because I looked in the mirror and noticed a dental issue. The rest was the inevitable unfolding of my interpretations of me, aging. Imagine what shows up when I walk into the Senior Center with all these unacknowledged thoughts and feeling? Like so many of us aging ageists, I spew all of my failings and my meaningless humiliation onto those innocent individuals that are my target of disdain, because they are just like me, and I'm just like them.

The practice of what psychologists call "projection", allows each of us to deny a personal emotional "truth" about ourselves, and only see it in those outside ourselves. That moment when I experienced and acknowledged my deepest failure, humiliation, and meaninglessness I was allowed to see what I normally just project onto most white-haired people, not with compassion but with judgment and contempt.

Aging and ageism resides within the eye of the beholder. Though projected out onto the external world, it usually has everything to do with one's own personal resistance to acknowledging and accepting the truth of who they are within these wrinkled, baggy, old bodies. It has absolutely nothing to do with those upon whom we impose judgments. We separate ourselves out, seeing ourselves being somehow different and better than others, even within our own age, race, class, sex, or political or religious positioning.

Aging like a guru requires that we take on the challenging task of being present and truthful with ourselves. I believe the hardest challenge of aging like a guru is to acknowledge that yes, indeed, in many ways we have failed. In many ways we have humiliated ourselves. In many ways our lives are not in alignment with what we imagined for ourselves. And, at times, life does seem meaningless. As we age like gurus we accept the truth of all of this and surrender the critical self-judgments that burden us with far more than just the aches and pains of everyday living.

As I examine the aging process, I am far more appreciative of what it takes for every individual to get out of bed every morning and face the unknowns of the day. Humility replaces humiliation. Meaning is found in the simpler parts of life, and failures are surrendered too. It takes courage to face every day, for all of us, not just those who are considered old and aging. We certainly aren't sissies!

Who me? Aging? Yes, I am!

Chapter 18

Dying – the Final Big Adventure!

We die a thousand deaths within one lifetime. We experience ourselves in untold numbers of transitions. We face the unknown at every stage of life, and it appears as though most of us have survived.

There is the deconstruction of our childhood as we immerse ourselves into puberty and adolescence; we leave behind adolescence when we choose careers, marriage, families – arenas of life where we grow our willingness to be accountable for our words and our actions. The death of innocence occurs over and over again, as reality shows us the ugly, the horrific, and all that has us question our sanity. Each of these crossroads brings us into a process of metamorphosis, within which we experience an undeniable transformation. The past becomes irrelevant. The future cannot yet be imagined. In this moment, we stand naked and free, strong, and willing to fly.

A Warrior and Defeat

Carolyn is transitioning. Vitality and vigor to fight her stage 4 cancer were the sword and shield she wielded. She had apparently been winning the battle for the past 2 years, but something shifted, and she has gone from seeing herself as unstoppable and unbeatable to an individual who hasn't the energy to walk, talk, or eat. She has transformed herself from everyone's champion to a frail human being, with the inability to even desire to do what it would take to be who she was just weeks ago. Carolyn is at the edge of her final frontier, experiencing the adventure of being Carolyn through this stage of life – her last stage.

My heart aches as I write this, because for me, this moment in Carolyn's life is truly one of the richest and poignant she will ever have an opportunity to experience. She could very well miss the achingly beautiful truth of who she is within this now fragile human form.

In our discussion group at the Senior Center, when the discussion of dying comes up, it is mostly regarding fear of the process being a painful one, with a lot of suffering. We anticipate the worst while we hope for the best. We spend countless hours and untold amounts of energy thinking about, imagining and worrying about the potential worse case scenarios of the end stages of life. Many would deny this to be the case, however; even Freud said that the fear of death influences us more than any other, even if it is on a sub-conscious level.

Most of us ignore our dying process as much as we ignore our aging process. We don't want to think about it, because it stresses us out! My friend, Shahiri, who has been at the side of many people as they transition from life to death, says that most people do the majority of their spiritual development in the last two weeks of their life. Why is this, you might ask? Because the inevitability of truth that is being experienced directly can no longer be denied.

When Carolyn received the prognosis from her oncologist, that there wasn't anything more they could do for her, she went home to be alone with herself. She isolated herself from her husband and her son. I imagined that she faced, for perhaps the first time, true defeat. And, with that, for any warrior, comes great humiliation and shame, because she failed to beat her cancer, she failed to beat death. I imagined that she also experienced guilt and self-hatred for abandoning her husband and son. Dying is a humbling experience, one that releases us from who we think we are, who we think we should be, and allows us to be fully open to who we are as our Divine, essential nature.

Dying is the process of transitioning out of this bodily form. For most people, it isn't death that is so frightening but this process of calmly dying, surrendering the fight, releasing the baggage that we have to leave behind, and heading out on another big adventure. Every one of us has a ticket for this grand experience.

Aging like a guru means observing how we engage with this (yet another) metamorphosis process, which is a very intimate and personal experience. What an opportunity to know oneself in a way that has yet to come our way. When the time comes, I hope that I will stay conscious, brave and open – kind of like keeping your eyes open on a roller-coaster ride – I don't want to miss a moment of it!

Chapter 19

Happiness Is an Inside Job

My client, Richard, is dying of lung cancer. He has had a rich life as a wealthy and successful brain surgeon; seems like Richard should be a happy guy too, right?

The truth is, for most of Richard's life, he was an unhappy alcoholic. Now, in his late 60's, he is retired, sober, and has just a few years left to live a happy life. Sitting in the middle of a crowded and noisy coffee shop, Richard asked me: "Rosie, how do I find happiness?"

I said: "Close your eyes, Richard, and think a happy thought." Within two seconds, a radiant smile came across his face. He opened his eye, which were now sparkling with delight. "Wow. That was easy!"

****

Meg is depressed, frustrated, and resists even trying to be happy. She sees happiness as overrated, because rarely does she see people happy, so why bother?

Meg has a BIG attachment to what happiness is supposed to be like, and it isn't happening for her or for most of the people she observes. However, the more attachments Meg has to how it's supposed to be, the less likely she'll be happy.

I asked her: "Meg, what needs to shift so that you may have more access to happiness?" Meg was quiet for a while. She looked angry, crossed her arms, closed her eyes and started to cry. "I'm so afraid to let myself even hope that I can feel happy. I'm resisting any possibility, because I don't want to feel more disappointment. I can see that I'd have to shift where I focus my attention – away from negative experiences. I'd have to train myself to focus on positive experiences. I'd have to shift my attention and the way I look at things, so my life is more positive." Meg smiled.

*****

Marjorie's five-year-old grandson, Troy, is visiting her for two weeks.

She has been looking for this quality time with Troy since her daughter announced she was pregnant with him many years ago. Instead of experiencing happiness, Marjorie is frustrated, worried, and full of anxiety: "I can't keep the house clean; my budget for Troy's visit is going really fast, and I can't take care of my business while I'm spending time with him. I feel stressed, and I'm not experiencing the happiness I anticipated."

Like with Richard, I encouraged Marjorie to close her eyes and imagine herself totally present with Troy, letting go of her worries and angst. She sighed a big sigh, smiled, and giggled. "I didn't think I could feel this good in such a quick conversation."

Yes, happiness is accessible within a blink of an eye, yet, for most of us, happiness is a fleeting experience – it's very hard to hold on to. In fact, the more you try to hold onto it the quicker it disappears. Instead of holding onto happiness, it's far more beneficial to practice letting go of thoughts that create something *other* than happiness.

What is happiness? Happiness is a quality of being that appears only when we are in the present moment. Happiness isn't a thought, however it is precipitated by thoughts. Pleasant thoughts provide us with the experience of happiness, as long as we sustain these happy thoughts.

Many of us believe that when we have what we want, then we will be happy. However, once people have what they want, they quickly lose the experience of happiness, as they begin to desire something else. We've been trained to believe that happiness comes from getting what we don't have from an external source, and so we continue to strive to get more and more and more.

Both Richard and Marjorie got what they wanted; however, neither were fulfilled or happy for more than brief moments. Why?

Happiness can't be experienced from the past or from the future – it can only be experienced in the present moment. But to stay in the present moment, each of us has to let go of thoughts that create negative emotional states.

The fact of the matter is that most of us are so used to thinking about what isn't happening, what isn't getting done, what we don't have, what we can't get, that we don't allow ourselves to be present in the moment with that which brings happiness to us. It comes down to this: We really don't want to stop thinking thoughts that give us a sense of control, so, rarely can people be happy!

When Richard closed his eyes and thought a happy thought, he may have remembered a special moment, the first smile of his new born baby son; or perhaps it was a memory of the fragrance of jasmine. Maybe he was imagining a wonderful event that was coming in the future. It doesn't matter what the source was. What is important is that Richard brought happiness into the present moment for himself.

Research has found that long-lasting happiness is more likely when we empower ourselves to give up our attachment to getting what we want from external sources. This requires empowering ourselves to immerse ourselves in discovering the source of happiness that is within us. Happiness is an inside job!

Marjorie contacted me after Troy went home. She shared that she experienced so much happiness once she surrendered her worries and anxiety. She focused her intentions on thoroughly enjoying every moment with Troy. Sometimes she had to work hard to keep the thoughts about work from interfering with her happiness, but she said it was well worth the effort.

Meg also shared with me that she has been practicing putting positive spins on any event or circumstance that she usually saw as negative. "I really didn't want to do this practice, but I figured that the worst that could happen is that I could feel good that I was right about life being negative and no happiness available. However, I found myself whistling a happy tune, and it made me smile. Maybe there is hope for me after all."

Richard passed away two years after our conversation about happiness. His children shared that he was a much happier man in the last couple of years of his life, and that he smiled far more than they ever remembered.

Aging like a guru means knowing that happiness is available 24/7. We can have it in a blink of an eye, but only if we are committed enough to being happy that we willingly let go of what creates something other than happy.

It takes practice, courage, and discipline to empower oneself to have the capacity to be happy; however, as Meg, Marjorie and Richard realized, it was so much more fun being happy than not.

Chapter 20

Do I Love My Life?

For years now, I've been aware that I wake up in the morning feeling slightly melancholy, with a small degree of anxiousness thrown in for good measure. I'm not depressed, though some might label it so. I just feel uninspired and unmotivated to jump out of bed. I guess the thought that runs parallel to these feelings is: *What's the point of my life for me? Sometimes, it just feels pointless*.

I delight when there are stimulations of some sort awaiting me, in which case I anticipate the day with enthusiasm. But when it feels like the "same old, same old," I'm challenged to love my life.

I know I'm not alone. I suspect the majority of people use some form of stimulation to get them moving and keep them moving in the right direction, whatever that means to them. However, in my commitment to recover my life from all the ways I've been avoiding my life, I no longer count on food, sex, money, alcohol, or love to bring pleasure and contentment to my life. However, I still love my coffee!!!

My practice is to stop relying on these externals strategies and substances, and focus on my internal guidance system for inspiration. Most of the time it works. Sometimes it doesn't – especially first thing in the morning. I'm ready for a change – no wait – I'm ready for Transformation!

The What's the Point / Pointlessness Syndrome

I've come to realize there are a number of elements to this *What's the point-ness/Pointlessness syndrome*. The first is related to the degree of value I place on my life. How does my life create value for me...does my life create value for me? I know that I love my work, my home, my family, and my friends. Yet, I don't love my life!

How can I love aspects of my life but not love my life in its totality? Can a person love their life completely? Can they really love it all? As a Transformational Life Coach, I'm saying YES – of course! Personally though, I question my ability to make it so. However, I believe in walking my talk, and practicing what I preach. So here I sit, contemplating why it is so dang hard to love my life.

The second element surfaced a couple of evenings ago while I was doing my dishes (probably 5 dishes in total). I didn't want to do the dishes, and threw a mini-tantrum. It was one of those what's the point moments. (I recognize that I have a lot of these what's the point moments.). I realized that I expected some reward for doing the dishes, which equates to being good, and doing good deserves a reward.

In the midst of this query regarding loving my life, I came to see that I held a life-long belief that rewards of any kind from the external world should be forthcoming when I do all the things I "should be" doing. I'm a good, kind, and loving person. I work hard, I'm responsible, I stay present and mindful to living a spiritual life, and I contribute to the well-being of the Planet as best I can. Where are my rewards?! What's the point of doing what I do if the promised rewards never arrive?

One More Element: Waiting

For most of us, we live in waiting – hoping that something or someone will come into our lives and transform it from drab and lifeless to amazing and spectacular. I see how, on some deep level, I continue to live my life in waiting. I'm waiting for my life to change into that life which I've anticipated forever. That life may never show up. That life may never manifest!

So what am I left with? What am I waiting for, when I know there is nothing to wait for? Sounds depressing but it's not, really. It's part of our human dilemma. Part of growing ourselves into ourselves by empowering ourselves to make those changes that inevitably lead to transformation and a loved life.

Yesterday, after immersing myself in some contemplativeness, I just sat and said to myself: "Okay, so what is the point of my life? If I'm here to experience humanness through this particular embodiment; if I'm here to learn and to grow, gathering lessons and wisdom along the way, why think myself unfortunate with what I've got? Why be condescending of this particular incarnation – as if I had a choice; as if there was a life that would somehow be better than this one? And, why expect rewards from external sources when what's really true is that rewards are intrinsic, entrenched in my being, and in any action I choose to take?" I like it when my kitchen is clean, when the laundry is done, when my emails are answered.... It feels good to have things done, though I might not want to do what it takes to make it so. I love serenity. I love all the ways that my life reflects my desire for peace and beauty. It's just hard work, and sometimes, I simply don't want to do it.

When I put it all together, I was able to see how my life is absolutely perfect for giving me everything I came here to experience – including failing to see those rewards I've received that are far beyond my expectations. I couldn't think of one thing to change, other than the belief that it should be different. Funnily enough, this last thought shifted my perspective enough that this morning I woke up a little less melancholy and anxious, and a little more content and grateful for the way that it is. Fascinating!

If you are aging like a guru, you know that it's important for us to experience fulfillment of our whole beings, while we are alive. I believe this to be the winning ticket, which gets every one of us into the bonus round of the game of LIFE! If I'm not willing to provide myself with a valued and rewarding life, how could I expect someone else to provide it for me?

The part of me that isn't aging like a guru still holds on to the belief that the external world should validate my existence: provide me with money, power, fame, beauty; however, if I cannot create contentment and serenity within myself, valuing and validating my own existence, I most likely won't truly create it through my interactions with the world outside me. And, as I've heard many times, if I haven't come to love my life, I will never allow myself to fully receive abundance in any form as truly mine. So goes the process of the paradigm shift.

I want everyone to experience the fulfillment of their human-spirit - to age like gurus. That's why I do the work I do: empowering people to empower themselves to have all of the richness and fun they are willing to have. Keep questioning reality, if you dare, experiment with thinking differently and doing differently, and see what possibilities show up.

Chapter 21

What I've Learned, Thus Far, in My Spiritual Journey

Transformation is not a one-stop shop. There's so many ways to transform and so many things to learn along the path. Here's what I've learned to be true, at least for myself over the past few years:

1. There is only one source of Currency/income. It may appear to come from your job, a personal or bank loan, an inheritance, or from your credit cards; but without the Universal Source of all that is, the currency would not be flowing from those sources.

If the currency you think you need is not forthcoming in the form you think is required, it's because you don't need it. What you may be needing is an opportunity to receive from the bounty of lessons that are continually being bestowed upon you. It's a clever disguise for getting creative and curious about what you are doing and who you are being in your life. It's also an opportunity to list some of the countless ways currency is flowing in your life, in this moment.

2. There is only one source of Love. It may appear to come, or not come, from parents, children, partners, community, but without the Universal Source of all that is, Love would not be flowing through these sources.

If the love you think you need is not forthcoming in the form you think is required, it's because you don't need it. What you may be needing is an opportunity to receive from the bounty of lessons that are continually being bestowed upon you. It's a clever disguise for getting creative and curious about what you are doing and who you are being in your life. It's also an opportunity to list some of the countless ways you are being loved, in this moment.

3. There is only one source of Beauty. It may appear to come from sunsets and sunrises, from beautiful clothing, cars, boats, and holiday destinations. But without the Universal Source of all that is, beauty would not be flowing through these sources.

If the beauty you think you need is not forthcoming in the form you think is required, it's because you don't need it. What you may be needing is an opportunity to receive from the bounty of lessons that are continually being bestowed upon you. It's a clever disguise for getting creative and curious about what you are doing and who you are being in your life. It's also an opportunity to list some of the countless ways you are being bathed in beauty in this moment.

4. There is only one source of Fulfillment of all of our desires and wants, our hopes, and our wishes. It may appear to be from stuff and accolades, acknowledgments and project completions, the children we've created, or the power we've derived. But without the Universal Source of all that is, fulfillment would not be flowing through these sources.

If the fulfillment you think you need is not forthcoming in the form you think is required, it's because you don't need it. What you may be needing is an opportunity to receive from the bounty of lessons that are continually being bestowed upon you. It's a clever disguise for getting creative and curious about what you are doing and who you are being in your life. It's also an opportunity to list some of the countless ways you are being immersed in fulfillment, in this moment.

5. There is only once source of Faith. It may appear to come through meditation, prayer, books and people, spiritual and religious traditions. And though the Universal Source of all that is never anywhere but here in this moment, it is up to me/you to re-source it. Nothing can bring us the faith that is required. No one can teach us how to live in faith. It can be pointed to, explained and discussed, but only you alone can experience faith and the richness that it brings.

If the faith you think you need is not forthcoming in the form you think is required, it's because you don't need it. What you may be needing is an opportunity to receive from the bounty of lessons that are continually being bestowed upon you. It's a clever disguise for getting creative and curious about what you are doing and who you are being in your life. It's also an opportunity to list some of the countless ways you are already living and being in faith.

My spiritual journey has me encounter the many trials and tribulations - that is a no-brainer, given that I've chosen this path called humanity. Meeting moments of hopelessness, powerlessness, and helplessness is required in order to sincerely experience the true essence of humanity – the raw, vulnerable, messiness to which I must surrender – if I'm ever to make progress in my spiritual evolution.

It's so good to share with you what I've learned over these past years; however, I'd be remiss if I didn't also share that I still feel powerless, hopeless, and helpless sometimes, and wish that living in faith wasn't so scary. But with lessons learned – one being that there will never be an end to them – I've come to live more in peace and acceptance that this human path is an exquisite adventure.

Chapter 22

I'm Grateful for My Teeth

In my thirties I was alone and depressed. I was in a bad relationship, living and working far away from my children on the edge of Canada in the Province of Nova Scotia. I isolated myself from anyone who could or would be a friend. Dark nights, crushing days; I had no idea that life could get any better for me.

I was a therapist at the time, supporting individuals and families recovering from drug and alcohol addictions. I loved my work. I loved my clients. And, because I was fairly new to the fields of therapy and addictions, I found my clients to be my best teachers. In fact, those that had been sober and working their Twelve Step program of AA, NA, or AL-ANON had something that I desperately wanted: Serenity.

While studying to be a marriage and family therapist, I learned a lot of valuable skills, tools, and theories related to being human, but serenity wasn't part of the curriculum. Here, in the outermost edge of the Atlantic Coast, I found a way out of those dark nights and crushing days.

On a cross-country trip back home to visit my parents in Detroit, I stopped for gas in New Brunswick. As I walked around a bit to stretch my legs, I came across an old fellow, sitting on the curb next to the restroom. He was drinking from a brown paper bag and his eyes were about as glassy as they could get. As I walked past him to go into the restroom, I smiled and said hello.

"Are those your real teeth?" he asked in sheer amazement. The very sound of his voice let me know he was from Newfoundland, a province of Canada that is known for its fishing and its wonderful people. To the question regarding the realness of my teeth, I responded "Yes, they are my real teeth." Slurred and blurry-eyed the man said "Well, you should count yourself very lucky. I don't know many women your age who still have their own teeth." I said thank you, with a big grin on my face and went inside the restroom. When I came out, he was gone.

I started reading literature on co-dependency. One of the most important foundations of any recovery program is the use of gratitude to find one's way to serenity and sobriety. With gratitude it is possible to re-frame being powerless and helpless into being healthy, vital, and accountable for your life. But you have to want something bad enough. Though I didn't know what it was I wanted, I saw it within many individuals in recovery. Even though their lives were full of challenges, they were happier than me. What's up with that? In my mind I rationalized that I should be happier than them. However that wasn't the case.

I started trying to list things I was grateful for. At that time, like I said, I had so much anger in me and I felt so victimized by life, my parents, and my boyfriend that, as hard as I tried to come up with things to be grateful for, I found more reasons not to be grateful. I had to keep asking myself, *"How badly do you want serenity?"*

As I lay in bed confronted with wanting both serenity and my righteousness, I remembered the old Newfoundland fellow saying I should feel lucky that I had my own teeth. That was the moment I got it. I got the value in the practice of gratitude. I got the degree to which I held onto a sense of entitlement; that life should be the way I think it should be. I got how much I take for granted: health, friends, a good job, a roof over my head. I began to think about how all my body parts work, all the time. That I have eyes that see and ears that hear. I can move my toes and feel my heart beating. In that moment, I became a very lucky person, and a very grateful person too.

Every night, I'd come to my gratitude practice as an angry, frustrated victim. Every night I struggled to find something to be grateful for. And, every night I came to remember my teeth, and how grateful I am that I have teeth. I also began to bring into my list of gratitudes the Newfoundland fellow. He gave me an amazing gift of realization. He gave me the first step toward serenity.

Developing a capacity for gratitude is like developing any muscle in our bodies. We have to first find it, perhaps discover it for the very first time.

That realization is just the beginning. Bringing conscious awareness to that muscle takes discipline and dedication – one moment at a time. And like any other capacity, gratitude never stops growing, and it never stops being an essential quality of being human and connecting us to the universal source of all that is.

AND, Life never stops throwing curve balls, but through practices such as listing things you are grateful for, you come to find that you can be with those curve balls with more peace and less frustration.

Recently, when I was facing some financial problems without much hope in sight, I said the prayer "Oh, Creator. Thank you for the way that it is." Initially I felt the rising up of the righteousness of my suffering. But soon after, I began to see all the gifts that were available to me, because I was having to be with these challenging circumstances. The wisdom of Creation revealed itself to me and I opened to a new level of gratitude. My capacity to see life different shifted dramatically in that moment and my life has never been the same.

I'm grateful that I have had the opportunities to experience wisdom and moments of enlightenment. I've been practicing aging like a guru since my 30's, and will continue until the moment my spirit leaves this bag of bones. If we are lucky enough, we all will be blessed with many people who out of the blue say one little sentence to you. And in that moment you know that you have been in the presence of a guru.

Chapter 23

No Peace on Earth

There will never be peace on Earth. Never! Not as long as humans put themselves in charge of the rightness and wrongness, the goodness and the badness, prosperity and poverty. Nope: It ain't gonna happen!

Peace will come when we give up doing unto ourselves and others what is hurtful, harmful, and destructive. I drink coffee and alcohol, use sugar and eat meat and wheat – all of which are destructive to my system. I use electronics, drive a fossil-fueled vehicle, and count on many of those organizations that contribute to the destruction of the planet to keep me safe and provide electricity, etc., for my comfort. Like the majority of individuals on the planet, 70% of my thoughts are negative. This also contributes to an internal environment that is not peace-full; it is actually dis-eased. I've been in relationships with people that cause me constant frustration as my expectations have me distance myself, withdraw, and withhold. I've felt victimized and wanted to get back at the individual who broke promises and ignored agreements. Yet, I say I want peace.

I have come to realize that the world doesn't need fixing – no peace required. It is perfect and faultless in providing an environment within which we learn and grow through the trials and tribulations of the circumstances we are presented. That is the whole deal with coming into human form and to Earth University; make all the classes easy and effortless and the learning disappears. Therefore, we need the world the way it is, until we need it another way, and then, it will miraculously become that!

From this Universal Consciousness/Spiritual Intelligence perspective, all corporations and business environments are also perfect for getting the learning we've come to get. Perfection is always and everywhere. It's up to us to get smart enough to recognize such perfection and utilize it for the very purpose for which it has presented itself.

My perspective, in this moment, is that we are here, enrolled in Earth School, from nursery school to post-graduate work. We are here to become enlightened to greater and greater degrees. There is no end to which one can become enlightened; learning opportunities just keep on coming. It's as if the more conscious and enlightened we become, the more the Universe creates a greater array of challenges for our species. Eckhart Tolle said that never before could a species consciously choose evolution. Evolution: Hmmmmm. Is there ever an end to evolution? I dare say there is none!

How do we evolve? We evolve only when we are at the edge of our comfort zone and are pushed, or voluntarily push that edge, to include what never before was possible, what could never be imagined and, what is now only a twinkle in our creator's eye! There is no limit to our evolution as long as we keep ourselves in the game.

Okay, so that sounds as if we can take ourselves out of the game. No, we can't. And you may think you want to because the game in some ways seems to be getting bigger than you, and scarier than you planned on. It may be; however, what's important is to focus on what's yours to do. What course are you currently in and what are the objectives of this particular learning opportunity? No, you can't take yourself out of the game, because, like a "Dalai Lama's hotdog," you are one with everything.

I believe that most of us have some investment in saving the planet – that somewhere in our personal or professional vision statement there's a word or phrase that reflects this compelling desire to do something to make this a better place for all of us. In the world of business, it's no different. Yet, we are challenged to do the job we are hired to do, at the same time attempting to cultivate an environment that is healthier to work in. At times we throw up our hands and whine "Is there no peace?"

As I began so I shall complete with "No; probably not." This doesn't mean that life will be full of despair, frustration, and depression – not any more than it has been up 'till now. So, we learn to be peaceful within, though the circumstances around us are not to our liking; we must find what causes a lack of peace. To age like a guru we ask ourselves what would be valuable to learn, discover, or practice in situations within which we feel out of control. This is how we cultivate peace – at least for moments at a time.

I retired from saving the Earth and all the people and beings that live here too. Sometime I forget that I retired, but when I remember it becomes clearer that what's mine to do, and what's only mine to do, is to let myself off the hook for only being human, which often includes being less than perfect, not fulfilling other people's expectations, and feeling guilty and shameful about my inadequacies and unworthiness. What's mine to do is to practice kindness towards myself and others and to be mindful of what I do that could be harmful; in effect, trying to minimize my impact on the earth.

I love peaceful moments and pray that all of us can share peace – if for only moments at a time. They are exquisite!

Chapter 24

Aging - What's the Point?

When I think about the millions of people who are in their 60's, 70's, 80's, and 90's, I wonder what brings fulfillment to their lives. As they disengage from the external world, by choice or by circumstance, most will question reality, much like Scarlett, Martin and Thomas do. Here is a snippet of conversation from our group, Aging-Who Me?

"When I was young," started Scarlett, who is a beautiful, vivacious 80-year-old woman, "everything mattered: what I looked like, what I wore, who I dated, where I lived, how many children I had, where they went to school. Everything mattered! I enjoyed waking up with a sense of purpose. Now I wake up and I miss feeling that energy that got me up in the morning. Now, I don't know what to get up for. I'm okay once I get started and get busy, but now, nothing matters, really."

Scarlett is not unusual. Those who are aging - like all of us, transition through stages of life from those times when everything makes sense and everything means something - through those times when nothing matters, and who cares anyways? What we think of as a mid-life crisis – that is typically thought to occur in one's 40's and 50's - is founded on the shattering of the illusion that what is significant should remain significant, and, what you want to be significant, isn't. We've been trained to believe in THE REALITY, and all of a sudden, it isn't. The opportunity to question reality and ask - What's the point? - confronts the world around us and the world within. This moment can be a huge game changer for individuals. And it is happening at all stages of aging; there is no longer that demarcation of when mid-life begins or ends.

Thomas asks: "Who came up with the concept of THE GOLDEN YEARS? What a crock of S**T!" Thomas is finding that what used to be significant and important in his life, like his favorite NBA team, or money, or ... just isn't important any more. He looked forward to being retired and to all the freedom that would give him. For Thomas, he knows that it isn't apathy he is feeling. It's just that what was significant to him in the past just doesn't matter anymore. So now what?

Martin chimes into this conversation. "For me, I find that I just don't care. And, I do feel apathy, like, *what's the point,* nothing matters anyway! I'm disappointed that these golden years suck in ways I hadn't ever imagined."

Purposelessness and meaninglessness confront Martin at the moment of awakening. He is racked with why's, what's, who's and when's. Martin finishes with: "When nothing matters, I'm like a rudderless boat leaving the dock: I don't know where I'm headed or how I'm going to get there. So I consider just staying at the dock, which means that more often than not, I'm staying in bed!"

As we age, so many of our identities that were critical to our sense of self fall away. I hear people say: "Who am I now that I'm retired, alone, arthritic? Who am I without my precious 'things' that used to be so important to me? Who am I in this moment with no purpose or meaning? Who am I in the midst of meaningless and purposeless?"

These aren't rhetorical question. Someone inside you - regardless of age, is asking the questions, because you want to get to know who is having the experience of aging, and is transitioning through various aspects of life. Who is having the direct experience as you - as the being within the experience?

Most of us are terrified to reflect on these questions. We avoid the emotionality that resides within. I believe that in the midst of the experience of meaninglessness is an opportunity to step into the true rich experience of this - this exploration that is as meaningful and fulfilling as any in the world.

Quite a few studies indicate that people die soon after retiring and soon after the death of a spouse or partner - it's called the widowhood effect. Our work, partners, and families bring meaning and fulfillment to our lives, or at least they are supposed to. It's where we create a sense of identity, meaning, and purpose. When we stop working, when our partners die, when families are less involved, people are more likely to give up and die. "What's the point of going on?" asks Martin.

Scarlett shares that though she isn't experiencing the excitement of engaging in her day as she had done in the past, once she gets up and busy, she is okay. I encourage Scarlett to stay in bed a little longer, and to be with that part of her that is experiencing a loss of meaning and purpose. I ask her to imagine herself back in bed being with herself, rather than avoiding herself. Because Scarlett is curious and fascinated with life, she easily sees the value of such a conversation with herself. She says, "I can do that! I see how this can be a richly valuable exercise for me - for anyone!"

Aging like a guru means that those phases of life, within which one may experience meaninglessness, purposelessness, feeling insignificant or valueless, doesn't have to lead to depression, which often leads to medication, isolation, and death at an earlier age. These phases provide opportunities to have deep and important conversations with yourself. These conversations allow each of us to make sense of our reality - the one we are currently in. These conversations are meaningful and purposeful, especially when the intention is to discover and reclaim the vibrancy of the living energy-being that you are - always!

The intention of this book is to cultivate curiosity and consciousness about who you are within - who lives in two worlds at once: the external world and the internal world. Creating dialogs with yourself can be challenging, and you may want to consider giving yourself some sessions with an individual who can support and companion you through this process of living with aging and change. There is wisdom in sharing yourself with those who know and understand the path and the journey of humanness. They can support and encourage you in your own unique process of aging like a guru!

Chapter 25

Stubborn and Pissed off - Who Me?

Carly

I'm working with a young woman, Carly, who is 15 years old. Her parents asked me to work with her because she is really frustrating to live with. They said she always seems to be unhappy, and her attitude is one of 'pissed-off-smarty-pants.' She believes she knows better than anyone else, and seems disgusted and judgmental about everything.

When first meeting Carly, she wouldn't look me. She hunkered into the corner of my couch with her big down jacket pulled around her securely. What I could only see was her jaws, aggressively chewing on a piece of hair hanging in front of her eyes.

Carly says "It's not my fault I'm this way. There's nothing I can do to please my parents, and so, I give up! In fact I'm going to make their lives as miserable as I can, because they have made my life a living HELL!"

Arnold

Visiting Arnold in his home, he sits in his Barcalounger, staring out the window. He doesn't want me there, and he doesn't want to talk.

"It's not my fault that I feel so crappy," says Arnold, who is 83 and suffering from many, many afflictions. "My children and my caregiver want me to be happier, get out more, and find friends. They say I would feel better. What do they know about me? They don't understand, and they don't seem to want to understand. They just want me to be different so they don't have to pay so much attention to me. Well, I'm going to make their lives a living HELL!"

The work I do as a life coach is to empower people who want to make changes in their lives; they willingly agree to participate in the process of fulfilling their goals - the ones they truly desire. This process takes self-discipline and self-accountability on the part of the client, and on my part too.

At first glance, Carly and Arnold are very much the opposite of my ideal client. Neither of them wanted to be with me. Both only wanted me to bug-off! They don't want to be anything but snarky, unavailable, and contemptuous. They figured I'd leave and let them continue to do what they do to make people go away.

But even though Carly and Arnold don't seem like my ideal clients, in one particular way, they are. Here is how that's true:

Very few people in the world are happy, peaceful, and content. Most people say they want to be happy but can't find their way clear of the obstacles to happiness. What is the obstacle that stands in their way?

Each of them, each of us, have a Carly and Arnold within us: a snarky, unavailable, contemptuous aspect of ourselves, who refuses to give up their attitude towards happiness. I see it all the time. And of course, I see it in myself as well. Who me?

Through our aging process, we have a multitude of opportunities to see those aspects of ourselves that interfere with truly enjoying life. We blame our circumstances, our parents, our political systems, our children, our bodies, . . . and the list goes on. As I mentioned in the chapter *Agism in the Aged - That's Wacky,* we project our unwanted "truths" about ourselves onto others. We don't want to own what is really true within ourselves for many, many reasons.

Attitudes are ways of being that we cultivate ourselves, because we want to – not because we have to. (Well, for some, they have to, but we will leave that for another time.)

In a class I took, called *Aging and Change*, at Wilfred Laurier University, the old and wise professor said constantly - only to make his point - "As people age, they become more of who they already are. If you are a happy person in your youth, you'll become happier as you age. If you are a grumpy person in your youth, you'll become grumpier as you age." These words have stuck with me for 35 years. I think about them when

I'm feeling grumpy, pissed off, and contemptuous of the world. In those moments, I recognize that I haven't let go of some of those people, places, and things that offended me in some way. I still hold a grudge against them. I still wish that things were different. And so, my ability to be happy is handicapped by my unwillingness to let go of what couldn't be, or wouldn't be, the way that I wanted.

We cultivate attitudes and behaviors that serve a specific outcome for ourselves. Carly wants to punish her parents. Arnold wants to punish his children and caretaker. Other people use love to get what they want, others use humor, others use their intellect, others use emotions, some use all of the above. We are trying to get something that feels impossible to get, given that we feel powerless. So, we manufacture attitudes and behaviors that we believe will get us what we want. Most of the time, however, it doesn't really work.

Though Carly was resistant to speak, when I asked her what she gets out of punishing her parents, I saw a little grimace cross her face. That little gesture spoke volumes! It reminded me of Dr. Seuss' Grinch, when he was conniving to get something he wanted. What does Carly want, enough that she would commit to being miserable while happily punishing her parents? It is most likely the same thing Arnold wants. It's the same thing so many of us want, enough that we destroy any possibility for fulfillment and happiness. What is that?

In a blog I wrote for my book Diet Like a Guru, I talked about how when we feel powerless, we empower ourselves the only way we can. We use substances, attitudes, and behaviors to get what we want, even if it's only on the inside. If making other people miserable gives someone a sense of power, it's probably what they learned to do, only to give themselves some sense of personal power. All of us, all of us, all of us do this, in one way or another! I can't emphasize this enough! No kidding Rosie!

People are brilliant when it comes to cultivating interpretations about life, and the survival strategies that align with those interpretations, especially when we are in our childhood. And, most of us still operate from those beliefs and interpretations, utilizing the same beliefs we created perhaps decades ago. Most of the time we don't even know we did this creating back then. That is why change is so difficult, because our ways of being in the world are so entrenched in how we hold those moments when we perceived circumstances a certain way, then made meaning about that moment, which often lasts a lifetime.

So what does this mean? It means Carly can grow herself into an Arnold, if she isn't willing to discover a different way to empower herself, other than to punish her parents.

And Arnold will continue to feel like a disempowered old guy until he owns his own reasons for wanting to punish the people who truly care about him. Both he and Carly empowered themselves to choose to be miserable and punishing. That tells me they have the capacity to empower themselves to choose something else - but only if they want to.

I'm pleased to report that both Carly and Arnold were able to talk about what was missing in their lives that had them want to use their power to punish others. Openly revealing one's truth is not only the first step but the most important step to cultivating a happier, more empowering relationship with oneself. At some point this does translate into creating happier relationships within the world we live in as well.

Aging like a guru is big, scary and hairy work, regardless of how old we are. It requires looking at how we use and abuse our personal power, which can be a humbling experience. But it is so, so worth the inner adventure!

Chapter 26

The Anguish and Agony of Unrelenting Resistance

I have a client, Max, who in this moment finds himself in a life that is unmanageable. Regardless of where he is - at work, at home, in his truck driving between home and work - he is facing what feels like cataclysmic consequences. It is as though he is attempting to walk through a field of land mines: whatever step he takes, regardless of the direction, it will inevitably result in a Ka-Boom!

. . . .

It is the end of pre-season for football. The athletes who have put their careers on the line to be chosen as one of the 53 players for any one of the NFL teams, face either a new beginning or the end of their dreams. If he fails to prove he is the best, he then faces the agony and anguish of defeat.

. . . .

A woman on the Island died of cancer last week. Her husband was left with unmanageable grief. He died three days later. It is not uncommon for people who have lost a spouse to die within months of each other, for they, like Max, face the depth of their humanity they perhaps have never experienced before. It is enough to drive one into what feels like insanity. It isn't insanity, however, it is just a place that has been avoided and ignored. No one wants to face such unutterable loss.

. . . .

As I write this, my friend Bryan joins me after taking a wonderful walk on Orcas. He shares with me that his family in Houston is about to experience flooding in their homes - that the waters are rising three inches an hour. The idea of life becoming unmanageable has now become a reality for close to six million people in Texas, and perhaps surrounding states.

In this moment, just like for Max, there is nowhere to go, nowhere to hide. It's just one big fat *be-with!*

I could go on mentioning a plethora of examples where people meet themselves, perhaps for the very first time, in the devastation of life and their dreams as they have been known. At some time or another in the process of aging, every one of us reaches such a state, where life is unmanageable. You recognize it by the degree of anguish you experience, the degree of resistance to accepting the isness of what is, and the degree to which you consternate about how to get out of both the experience of powerless-hopeless-helpless and the circumstances that triggered it. When your home, car and business are flooded, how the HELL do you be with all *that?*

As we age we inevitably face certain life crises that affect how we experience both our humanness and our spiritual-ness. There is no way out of the many life-transitions that are incurred over the decades of being human. It just is part of the isness of being in a human suit. No one is given the Rand McNally Maps of the Universe. Inevitably, each one of us gets lost. Each one of us comes to the chasm and the abyssness of their life, where there is no way out and nothing left to do but surrender completely to the truth that: "This is bigger than me and I, in this moment, am powerless. I surrender."

Anyone who has attended a 12-step program knows the reality of this moment of experiencing powerlessness in the midst of the truth that life has become unmanageable. It's the first step out of the field of land mines. Max has been here before and is here again, and being that he is only in his 40's, he may have more opportunities to find himself in the unmanageable reality of land mines. He laments: "Why is this happening to me? I must have done something bad and very, very wrong."

No one has done anything wrong, though we have been trained to think this way. It's just that we forget that we are human beings having a human experience - one that stretches our courage and faith to acknowledge when life feels too big, too hard, and too scary to face. It is not a bad thing at all to admit defeat, powerlessness, and that life in this moment is unmanageable. I know for myself and for thousands of people I've spoken to who've admitted that this is where they are, there is relief in giving up the belief that they are in control. In this moment there is a shift, and in this shift there is an experience of returning to sanity.

What to Do When There Is Nothing to Do

Our culture is one of doing. In the midst of any circumstance that creates a sense of crisis, emergency, or cataclysm, we look for what can be done to feel empowered and in control, in the midst of a disempowered reality.

Max and just about everyone else on the planet put up tremendous resistance to letting go of the doing in order to surrender into the moment of being human - nowhere to go and nothing to do. But this is what it takes to age like a guru, and it goes against all the training we've ever been given. To admit defeat is devastating to our egos. To admit defeat is an opening to our humanness. To admit defeat expands awareness through the experience of humility and humbleness. Empowering oneself to age like a guru, to admit defeat and powerlessness allows the human being to be recognized and experienced fully. To our ego-self, this is death. To our human-spirit it is a wha-hooo!

It is empowering to admit that you are at the end of your rope. To surrender control and one's will to have things turn out the way that "it's supposed to" is tremendously difficult, especially if there is no one who we believe we can trust, who we can turn to, and turn things over to. Though the U.S. is founded on the principle of "In God We Trust," it isn't how we orient ourselves in everyday life, in the midst of ordinary cataclysms. This is indeed a dilemma. So many of us feel stuck because we are afraid to admit defeat and to actually have the human experience of defeat and powerlessness.

And so we sit in a field of land mines hoping someone will come to rescue us, when the truth is that, perhaps with the support of others who are familiar and comfortable with these life experiences, we can learn how to rescue ourselves from ourselves. Life isn't always easy and it's not always fun, but oh, what a brilliant opportunity to learn to be you! That is what aging like a guru is all about!

Chapter 27

The Potentiality of No Buts

I woke up this morning by Gracie tapping her little furry paw on my chest. She's ready for the day to begin - I'm not. I feel into the sense of lacking - my orientation in life is that I'm always lacking something - what is it this morning? (Can you imagine waking up next to this person who is always lacking and anticipating a day created from lack - not fun, right?) And this is what inspired this writing. Cool, eh?

I'm graced with the ability to cultivate greater degrees of awareness regarding how I'm choosing what I choose. The truth is, we are all graced with this ability. I just happen to be fascinated by the human dilemmas that face us all - enough that I keep diving deep into those aspects of humanity that keep most of us stuck, stymied, and settling for a life that is less than outstanding. I want to know how to get out of this 'less-than' orientation and create for myself, and perhaps inspire others too, to see the potentiality we are immersed in. Potentiality for what? Here are some examples that perhaps points to the potentiality for what:

*** I've been teaching myself to draw portraits with colored pencils, and I need to buy some supplies that could make the process more enjoyable and effective. I say to myself: "Well, I don't know how committed I am to this particular medium. I don't want to buy something and only use it once or twice. What if it doesn't work well and I've wasted that money? ($20!) What if I abandon colored pencils altogether?"

So I struggle more because I choose to use less, thus missing out on the potential of enjoying and excelling in this medium.

*** I've lived in a small travel trailer for over 13 years, which works fine enough. All my needs are met - warmth, comfort, freedom from a burdensome mortgage, and more. When I imagine the house I'd like to build, I say to myself: "Well, you are old - how long would you live in a house like that anyway (Only for about 30 years)? And, besides, with global warming, weather changes and all, that house may be destroyed before you get a chance to live in it. You like being environmentally friendly, keeping your footprint of existence small - do you really care about the environment? You don't need more - you're good with what you got."

So I continue to live in my tiny trailer, longing for room for - yes, an art studio, among other things. I miss out on the potential for creating space that will give me greater degrees of ease, comfort, and beauty.

*** My friends Heather and Bryan Benepe, and their daughter Zoey, have invited me to visit them in Bali, and to stay for as long as I'd like. They have a hotel there, right on the beach. I could snorkel, work on my books, paint, and rest. I could also continue to work with clients over the phone, and perhaps provide a workshop or retreat. What an amazing opportunity, eh? But I say to myself: "Well, what if I don't like it, what if it's too noisy, what about my job at the Center, I'll miss Gracie - she'll miss me! It's hot and humid in Bali - I don't like hot and humid. What if a huge storm blows through the Pacific Northwest and destroys my home?"

So I dither and consider all of the potentially bad consequences that could ruin my life by going to Bali, and by doing so, I miss out on the potential for unimaginably wonderful things to happen because I went to Bali.

*** I haven't had a partner for over five years. I imagine enjoying the company and partnership of someone who laughs a lot, loves to cook, is warm, sweet, adoring and affectionate - okay, I'll say it - a soulmate! But then, I say to myself: "Well, you are really happier on your own; you don't like sleeping with anyone; and you know it will most likely turn out like all the other relationships in your life. It's too much of a pain when there are disagreements."

So I miss out on the potential of even meeting a guy who might just want to be friends and share some life experiences together. I miss out on actually experiencing directly what I only allow myself to imagine for mere moments at a time.

Can you hear the pattern?

Through my teaching, coaching, and my life and spiritual practices,

I encourage people to explore how they are choosing to choose to create their lives. In this moment I examine how I chose to create my own life, and, much like my clients, I notice that I am afraid of making mistakes.

I won't let myself have what I want; I only let myself have what I need. I look at what I don't want - to waste money, time, and energies. The question that underlies all the dilemmas above is - *What if I don't want what I think I want - what if I'm wrong again?!* That means that I have wasted valuable resources, money, time, and energy. Most of us waste these resources all the time and think nothing of it. By focusing on the potential of wasting time, money, and resources, I just keep missing out on realizing the potentially positive moments of even just saying - this is what I want!

I take a deep breath and feel into the discomfort of the probability of getting it wrong. What are the consequences of living within my needs and not my desires? What if I only let myself want what I know I can have?

My mind constantly attempts to justify my heart's desires. Truth is, I'd most likely have a much more fulfilling life if I didn't let my head have a say in the whole thing. I've been taught that ignoring reason and logic is very dangerous. That's so fascinating, given that the potentiality of all the amazing inventions that make our world as wonderful as it is began with ignoring reason. We are not supposed to be able to fly, right?

But here is the thing: In this moment, all I want to practice is allowing myself to say just to myself - "Here's what I want!" Tears well up, my throat closes down. Then, my mind says: "What the Hell is going on?! It's just a thought, for GOD's SAKES! Get over it!!!"

My experience is that this is where most of us live - in the "I want it, but...," and in the "if only." Quite often, when a client is sharing with me what they want, it is always followed by, "but I can't have it because..." I get paid the big bucks to say to these individuals: "Just say what you want, leaving off the 'but!'" Wow! It is hard work to leave off the 'but.' More times than you would imagine, my clients also end up in tears and feel choked up by just saying what they want out loud - no buts! Try it for yourself!

My commitment, in this moment, is to just allow desires to arise, without the need to act on them (a big element of our humanness is that we believe we have to act on everything, or justify why not to act). I'm curious to experience the potential of what could show up by just allowing desires without the 'buts.' Already my mind is creating stuff to derail this commitment. Jeesh!

The Rolling Stones sang, "You can't always get what you want." The truth is that if you don't let yourself want and desire, you will never get what you want. You will never get what you want!

If you want to age like a guru, the point is that we will never realize the potential of saying, "yes, this is what I want," if we never allow ourselves to truly know what we want, and to say what we want. The potentiality of possibility is lost.

In the aftermath of horrendous hurricanes, as millions of people experience the loss of what they had, including safety, security, and stability, we realize that we can no longer justify ignoring our true desires, the ones that dreams are made of, for the sake of maintaining the illusion of safety and security. It is all up for grabs. Nothing is secure; nothing is for sure, except for the potential to create a life worth living.

As for me, I don't know if I'll get a house, a soulmate, a holiday in Bali, or new art tools. I only intend to experiment and witness the outcome of allowing the possibility of desires to show themselves - and they will show themselves!

Chapter 28

You Can Put Your Faith in That

All day long we process and interpret patterns and momentary snapshots of life, in order to make meaning. Tarot cards, astrology, economic forecasting, political unrest, weather patterns, a grumpy barista, getting up on the wrong side of the bed - each of us are continually bombarded with thoughts, sensations and emotions, all of which contribute to the ongoing practice of making meaning of our lives.

Making meaning gives us a sense of who we are in the midst of the reality we are immersed in. Making meaning also provides a sense of safety, security, stability and invulnerability. We continually look for what makes sense in the world and what we can put our faith in. Yes, meaning and faith are intricately and intimately connected!

When an individual cannot make meaning of the circumstance in front of them, they begin to lose faith in themselves and their reality. They feel vulnerable, exposed, and uncertain of who they are and what is theirs to do. They doubt their ability to function in the real world, and they begin to lose faith. They are afraid to tell anyone what it is like inside them, because they believe they are the only one to ever experience a crisis of faith, more widely thought of as a mid-life crisis.

Generally, when in a midlife crisis, the experience is - 'my life has no meaning,' and uncertainty and doubt arise. People feel directionless and lost. Hope becomes hopeless, and powerful shifts to powerless. Why? Because what we believed to be meaningful is now experienced as meaningless. What happened?

We think of a mid-life crisis as a crossroad. An individual arrives at this crossroad when what they think and what they do seem to be meaningless. When someone finds themselves at this juncture in life, he or she will use Herculean strength to stay on the well-worn path of normal. However, the true direction to experiencing personal meaning is to take that path less traveled. Choosing to fully immerse oneself into the experience of meaninglessness, though sounds intolerable, actually becomes the most empowering and exquisitely excruciating act of courage known to humankind. Yep, you read that right.

Since the aging process includes a whole lifetime, and because we are living longer than ever before, it isn't unusual for individuals to experience more than one life crisis. Adolescents question life and meaning, so much so that suicide is the second leading cause of death for children between the ages of 10 and 24. We are familiar with mid-life crises for those in their 30's, 40's, 50's. And, we know that for the elderly, the question of meaning is sometimes insurmountable. I just read that an elderly person is more likely to be successful at suicide than any other age group. Hmmm!

Sometimes a life crisis is a consequence of an event or circumstance, but more often than not, it occurs because there was a question that arose from apparently nowhere - "What does all of this mean?"

Quite often, regardless of the age of the individual, the experience is one of a shattering, as though the mirror on the wall that reflected their identity, their reality, fell and shattered into a million pieces.

Though this event can be as devastating as a full on car-crash, this shattering rarely involves an ambulance, or any other form of emergency medical assistance. This event quite often is never even talked about, though the internal experience can be horrific. Meaning, identity, purpose, values, priorities, beliefs, reality - all are obliterated! In this moment we are not only in a mid-life crisis, we are in a spiritual crisis - a crisis of faith.

Crisis of Faith

Up until this shattering, every single second of our lives we put all of our faith in the reality we trained ourselves to obey and to pay homage to. Rarely do we realize this is a practice of faith - one we don't even question.

Though we may go to church and say we put our faith in God, rarely do we put our faith in God during the week. Instead, we put our faith in our car, in our job, in our 401K, in the stock market, in our children, their teachers, the washing machine. We put our faith in our body, in alcohol, and other substances. We put our faith in doctors, hospitals, insurance companies, the media, and in our Facebook friends. Boy - I'm feeling agitated just writing this. I think I'll change the subject! Oh, I so want to let myself off the hook right now! But alas, I have a job to complete....

Aging like a guru isn't about the decline of our bodies and our minds. It's about cultivating wisdom. For me, wisdom is the ability to utilize the intelligence within us. Sadly this intelligence is sorely invalidated by the world we have immersed ourselves in.

We train ourselves to ignore our intelligence and our own personal experiences for what we are told. Instead we've trained ourselves to put our faith in our parents, teachers, and others we've deemed to be the authorities. A crisis of faith is the moment when we are required to reclaim our own ignored truths and intelligence. A crisis of faith requires a rehabilitation and strengthening of those muscles of self-trust, self-honor, and dignity.

By choosing to age like a guru, you cultivate trust and faith in your own direct experience as a participant of life; choosing to choose for yourself what something means, and choosing where to put your faith, based on your own experience - not someone else's.

You know when something has meaning for you, because in that moment you experience an uplifting sensation accompanied by a sigh of relief, as does the feeling of relaxation. You feel good - you might even find yourself smiling. You see beauty and light when perhaps just moments ago, all seemed in despair and ruin. In this moment you know what is true. The experience of delight intrinsic in this knowing, well, believe it or not, you can put your faith in that!

Chapter 29

Getting the Job Done Without Trying

This week my friend Marj had a second knee replaced, just ten months after her first knee operation. She is coming home today just two days after the surgery. Amazing. There is no dilly-dallying these days when it comes to hospital recuperation time. They expect you to get in, get out, and back on your feet the very same day as the knee replacement.

Marj went into both knee replacements with conviction and commitment that she would bring her A-Game. She exercised, changed her diet, went to Physical Therapy before and after the surgery of the first knee, and has been disciplined to make sure all goes the same with the second. And thus far, the results have been stellar! Less pain, more strength and mobility, and the ability to get to those events that make Marj's heart sing – literally. Singing makes her heart soar!

Marj is committed to her well-being, enough that nothing interferes with her appointments with herself for exercise, PT, and other aspects of her health practices. Yes – appointments with herself. In her heart, she knows that she wants freedom and flexibility, so much so that she is totally dedicated to doing whatever it takes to bring that to her. Is she scared that there are risks and discomfort? Yes. Does she know for a fact that the outcome of the surgery will be amazing? No. However, the outcome isn't the trajectory. Being present and bringing her All to every exercise session and PT appointment, sticking to the regimen required by the hospital; the completion of each aspect of her recovery program is what matters – not missing one single knee bend.

Marj didn't "try" to do her exercises, get to PT, and eat different. She totally committed herself to getting the job done and getting back into her life as quickly as possible, and with as much ease as came naturally. I'm impressed!

Throughout the aging process, there are many opportunities to try, and many opportunities to do. As a Life Coach, my experience – which includes my own, is that we are much more likely to try to make our lives better than to actually make our lives better. One of my clients who is in a 12-step program shared the slogan "Trying is Lying." Ouch! That hits home!

Trying smacks of hesitancy, resistance, and the unwillingness to fully commit to, and be fully accountable to your word. In a sense, when people try, they are usually juggling conflicting or underlying commitments. They want what they say they want, while at the same time, they want something else that may not have been verbalized yet.

Generally speaking, what most of us want is pain-free, vulnerable-free, comfortable, stability, safety and security. Wha-hooo! And, at the same time we want something that makes our hearts soar, and, will inevitably stretch our comfort zone. Any change brings about the fear of loss. Every change will also stretch an individual to consider if what is at stake is worth the loss and the gain. The practice of trying versus committing allows us to hedge our bets in favor of safety and invulnerability.

There are areas in Marj's life where she isn't as committed to bringing her best self to the endeavor. She is more committed to not letting go of comfort, stability, and the invulnerability that comes along with maintaining the status quo. She, like so many of us, believes that she would be sacrificing and depriving herself of comfort and safety if she gave up what she doesn't want to lose. It's fascinating to witness people like Marj be so brave and strong in one area of life, and be scared and hesitant in another.

The truth is that when you're absolutely clear about what you are committed to, you realize that you are sacrificing or depriving yourself of nothing. If you give yourself exactly what you want – where's the sacrifice in that?

Trying allows us to work at cross purposes with our inner truth. It sets the stage for sabotage of our own best efforts. The more we try the further away we get from that which we truly desire. Obviously, you don't have to take my word for it. Take an inventory of all the times in your life when you told yourself or someone else "I'll try." What was the success rate for you trying? And, if there were times that you committed to something and said, "I'll do it," what was the rate of success for saying YES?

When in doubt about the degree to which I want what I want, I often go to one of my favorite spiritual teachers: Yoda. Yoda's wise words in Star Wars, when he is training Luke Skywalker to be a Jedi, reveal a true aging guru: "Do or Do Not. There is No Try."

By the way, Marj is stronger and more capable on her first day home then she ever thought possible. Her commitment and discipline paid off for her, big time!

Chapter 30

The Everyday Gurus Among Us

John is a guru – not that he would recognize himself as one. He is in his mid-80's, retired, and lives with his wife Eleanor.

When looking at John, you wouldn't notice anything special about him, other than he is very tall, and when he smiles he lights up the room. He doesn't talk the spiritual talk, nor would he consider himself to be walking a path of spirituality. Yet, I find that when I'm around John, I'm relaxed, peaceful, and I'm not inclined to do anything other than just sit in his presence.

Hendrick is another guru. There is a different quality of presence in Hendrick than in John, but the delight I feel when I'm in his presence is palpable.

More and more I find within myself a greater capacity to recognize the gurus among us. They are just human beings living one day at a time, experiencing life issues the same as everyone else.

Guru's are like that. They are normal men, women, and children, and though they may have abilities to experience love and light beyond what most of us experience, their greatest gift is that, in their presence, people experience peace within themselves. In their presence, people enjoy being.

Can I Enjoy Being Me?

Most of the individuals who contact me for support and coaching have been immersing themselves in environments and relationships within which they don't enjoy being themselves. They, like most of us, think it's normal to struggle and be unsatisfied with life to one degree or another, regardless of a dream to have it be different. They complain and whine, and often talk about what's wrong with the world and what is wrong with themselves. I have to ask them the question: "When do you enjoy being you?"

When Do You Enjoy Being You?

You can't imagine the looks I get when I ask this question. It's as if the screen on one's computer just went blue – and then the reboot begins. They will say: "What do you mean, when do I enjoy myself?" Or, "Well, I'm not sure how to answer that question." They are stalling while they get a handle on what I'm asking. I get it. Few of us are comfortable knowing who we are – and what is true for us – inside our skin.

I, like so many people, initially found it unnatural to think or to know when I was enjoying myself, until my own therapist, many years ago, turned me in the direction of when, where, and with whom I enjoyed being me. My life then was primarily made up of relationships within which I thought I was supposed to be okay in. I worked hard to like and love people who didn't like or love me, nor had the capacity to love or like me, or themselves for that matter. I exhausted myself trying to be one who would be loved by everyone – especially by my mom and dad, sisters and brothers, husband and children. Truth is, no matter what, I rarely enjoyed being with them. Get it? I didn't enjoy being me – with them. But, because I was supposed to enjoy being with them, I figured there was something wrong with me, and I would never have what it takes to be happy, content, or fulfilled in any relationship. However....

I realized that there were times, people, places, and activities within which I thoroughly enjoy being me. Initially I made that wrong. But over decades, I've enjoyed being me as I am, wherever I am, even though I still sometimes judge myself, because my life looks different, quirky – anything but normal. I was trained to not like my life as it is; I'm supposed to be striving for better, different, more! But I'm giving up striving for better, different, more, and now only strive for simple acceptance of me as I am – no matter what.

As I strive for simple acceptance of me, I meet the most amazing people who are everyday gurus, who somehow, magically it seems, light me up, just by being themselves. I feel the warm embrace of connection, not by some special individual sitting cross-legged on a pillow, chanting OM.

No, these gurus are the clerks at the grocery store and friends around the kitchen table – sharing a meal and a game of cards. In these environments, with these people, which now seems like everywhere, I enjoy being, and I enjoy being me.

The upside of aging is that, as long as we are alive in these bodies, we are provided with opportunities to discover and embrace the being within. And, as we accept and enjoy the truth of this being within, more and more often those gurus magically show up in our lives, and we feel blessed, delighted, and enjoy just being. And then, my friends, you will have discovered the aging guru within.

Chapter 31

A Comma, Not a Period

I want to leave my life feeling ragged and worn out. I want there to be nothing left to be finished, nothing left to be said. I want to die with love in my heart. I want to be delighted with my accomplishments and forgiving of my mistakes.

Like my life, this book is unfinished. I have more to experience, to create, and to express as a human being. My writing of aging and life in general will go on and on, until I find I have nothing more to say. And with that, I send each of you love and light, and courage and strength to be curious and compassionate with yourself and others as we experience and learn from this temporary and magnificent journey of being human.

Acknowledgements

This Guru Series - to Parent, Diet and Aging Like a Guru began about two years ago, when, with the help of my dear friend Marj Franke, I began to create video blogs in service to parents in need of quick access to answers about parenting (Check out www.parentlikeaguru.com). After completing that series of Vlogs, we were inspired to talk about issues raised by every dieter, and thus was born Diet Like a Guru (www.dietlikeaguru.com). Aging Like a Guru never made it to Vlog status, but was a weekly article in Orcas Issues (www.orcasissues.com).

I'm most grateful to Marj for assisting me with patience and enthusiasm, not only by being the woman behind the camera, but by asking those questions that are asked by parent, grandparents, dieters and those of us who are aging. This series of books truly wouldn't exist without you, Marj!

Fred Franke, Marj's husband and my very good friend, read and edited so many of these blogs and vlogs. He is very picky in what he is willing to read, so I always felt honored and blessed by his willingness to read each piece that went into these books. Thank you Fred!

My support team, Ruby Hernandez who edits everything I write, and Maureen K. O'Neill, who has created and designed my covers, and formatted the past eight books - I so appreciate the clarity of presence that it takes to make words and pictures into a live, beautiful expression of being. Thank you both so very much!

Bio

Dr. Rosie focused her studies in Marriage, Family and Child Therapy in the 80's. In the 90's she focused on Spiritual Guidance and received her Ph.D. in Transpersonal Psychology. In 2000, she began integrating human/family dynamics with transpersonal and spiritual dynamics, creating and facilitating the Transformational Coaching Training Program through ITP, now Sofia University.

Dr. Rosie is considered a preeminent thought-leader in the field of Transformational Coaching. Her interests and passions have taken her from boardrooms to ashrams, all over the world, in service to supporting every individual to come into the fulfillment of their human-spirit. She has cultivated the capacity to soar alongside the most elite spiritual teachers in the world.

For more information about Dr. Rosie, visit: www.theparadigmshifts.com

More Books by Dr. Rosie Kuhn

Parent Like a Guru

Diet Like a Guru

Cultivating Spirituality in Children: 101 Ways to Make Every Child's Spirit Soar

ME: 101 Indispensable Insights I Didn't Get In Therapy

IF ONLY MY MOTHER HAD TOLD ME... (OR MAYBE I JUST WASN'T LISTENING.)

YOU KNOW YOU ARE TRANSFORMING WHEN...

DILEMMAS OF BEING IN BUSINESS

THE ABCS OF SPIRITUALITY IN BUSINESS

SELF EMPOWERMENT 101

THE UNHOLY PATH OF A RELUCTANT ADVENTURER

Please visit http://www.TheParadigmShifts.com for more information. To purchase books go to Amazon.com.

CPSIA information can be obtained
at www.ICGtesting.com
Printed in the USA
FFHW010453270119
50276881-55292FF